A Gift for

....

From

....

Date

....

D1058941

And this shall be a sign unto you; Ye shall find the babe wrapped in swaddling clothes, lying in a manger. And suddenly there was with the angel a multitude of the heavenly host praising God, and saying, Glory to God in the highest, and on earth peace, good will toward men. And the shepherds returned, glorifying and praising God for all the things that they had heard and seen, as it was told unto them.

LUKE 2:12–14, 20

When [the wise men] saw the star, they rejoiced with exceeding great joy. And when they were come into the house, they saw the young child with Mary his mother, and fell down, and worshipped him: and when they had opened their treasures, they presented unto him gifts; gold, and frankincense and myrrh.

MATTHEW 2:10–11

Now he that ministereth seed to the sower both minister bread for your food, and multiply your seed sown, and increase the fruits of your righteousness; Being enriched in every thing to all bountifulness, which causeth through us thanksgiving to God.

2 CORINTHIANS 9:10–11

WANDA E. BRUNSTETTER'S

Amish Friends CHRISTMAS COOKBOOK

BARBOUR BOOKS

An Imprint of Barbour Publishing, Inc.

Published by Barbour Books, an imprint of Barbour Publishing, Inc., P.O. Box 719, Uhrichsville, Ohio 44683, www.barbourbooks.com

Our mission is to publish and distribute inspirational products offering exceptional value and biblical encouragement to the masses.

Member of the
Evangelical Christian
Publishers Association

Printed in China.

Contents

A Brief History of the Amish and Mennonites

The Amish and Mennonites are direct descendants of the Anabaptists, a group that emerged from the Reformation in Switzerland in 1525 and developed separately in Holland a few years later. Most Anabaptists eventually became identified as Mennonites, after a prominent Dutch leader named Menno Simons. The word *Amish* comes from Jacob Ammann, an influential leader who in 1693 led a group that separated from the Mennonite churches.

Driven by persecution from their homes in Switzerland and Germany, both Mennonites and Amish began to immigrate to North America. William Penn welcomed them to Pennsylvania in the mid-nineteenth century, where many settled and then migrated into Ohio, Indiana, Iowa, and other parts of the country.

Both the Amish and Mennonites believe in the authority of the scriptures, and their willingness to stand apart from the rest of the world shows through their simple, plain way of living.

An Amish Christmas

Christmas is the most important holiday celebrated by the Amish—or, it should be said the Amish church groups that do celebrations of any kind, as a few very strict Old Order groups do not celebrate much of anything. Some Amish communities tend to be more stringent and traditional in their Christmas celebrations than those from the more liberal districts. Also celebrations will vary, depending on what part of the country the Amish family lives in. However, among all Old Order Amish, Christmas trees, twinkly colored lights, and Santa Claus are considered frivolous and worldly. They believe that Christmas should be celebrated with modesty and by focusing on the true meaning of Christmas—the birth of Jesus Christ, God's Son and Savior of the world.

While much time is devoted to prayer, meditation, and scripture readings, Christmas Day is spent fellowshiping with family, while giving thanks for the birth of Christ. It's also a time when Amish families get together for dinner and a gift exchange. It's a day of laughter and relaxation for all.

Although most Amish communities don't have a church service on Christmas Day, unless it falls on a Sunday, if Christmas comes near the end of the week, some Amish districts will hold their services on Christmas morning instead of the usual Sunday service. The Christmas church service follows the same pattern as a regular Sunday morning service, with the scriptures and messages emphasizing the importance of Jesus' birth.

> *Pleasant words are as an honeycomb,*
> *sweet to the soul, and health to the bones.*
> PROVERBS 16:24

Snacks and Bites

The best preparation for tomorrow
is to give life your best today.

Appetizer Roll-Ups

12 ounces cream cheese, softened
4 teaspoons dill weed
¼ cup thinly sliced green onions
½ pound each thinly sliced ham and turkey

Combine cream cheese, dill weed, and onions in mixing bowl.
Spread about 2 tablespoons on each slice of ham and turkey. Roll
up tightly and wrap in plastic wrap. Refrigerate overnight. Slice into
1½-inch pieces. Yield: 6 to 7 dozen.

SHARON KNEPP
Chouteau, OK

Tortilla Roll-Ups

8 ounces cream cheese
8 ounces sour cream
½ cup salsa
½ teaspoon seasoning salt
½ teaspoon garlic powder
½ to 1 cup shredded cheese
1 (8 ounce) package thinly sliced ham, cut up
12 (8 inch) soft tortilla shells

In a bowl, mix ingredients together in order given and spread on soft
tortilla shells to ¾ inch from edge. Roll tightly and slice them into
1¼-inch slices. Good to eat with salsa.

MARY ALICE YODER
Topeka, IN

GELATIN ROLL-UPS

1¼ cups boiling water
2 (6 ounce) boxes gelatin, any flavor
2 cups mini marshmallows

Mix water and gelatin together in a bowl until dissolved; then add marshmallows and stir until melted. Pour in large cookie sheet and refrigerate until set. Next, cut gelatin in half lengthwise; then cut 1-inch strips crosswise.

FILLING:
4 ounces cream cheese, softened
1 cup whipped topping
½ to ¾ cup powdered sugar

Mix cream cheese, whipped topping, and powdered sugar, and spread filling on top of cut gelatin. Let set to chill and then roll up the 1-inch strips.

"They look nice and are very tasty! These are usually a 'hit' at Christmas gatherings with all the sweet stuff!"

DORIS SCHLABACH
Goshen, IN

BACON-WRAPPED WATER CHESTNUTS

2 or 3 cans whole water chestnuts, drained
1 pound bacon strips cut into thirds
1 cup brown sugar
¾ cup ketchup
¾ cup Miracle Whip salad dressing

Set oven to broil at 425 degrees. Wrap a bacon piece around a water chestnut and secure bacon in place with a toothpick. Repeat with all water chestnuts. Place on a broiler pan and broil for 20 minutes. Remove from broiler pan and place in 9x13-inch pan. In a bowl, mix brown sugar, ketchup, and dressing together and pour over chestnuts and bake at 425 degrees for 20 minutes.

ELSIE MAST
Shiloh, OH

Low-Calorie Vegetable Dip

◇◇◇

2 cups cottage cheese
2 teaspoons instant beef bouillon
2 teaspoons minced dried onion
3 teaspoons lemon juice
1 (14 ounce) jar processed cheese (optional)

In a bowl, mix cottage cheese, bouillon, dried onion, and lemon juice until smooth. If processed cheese is used, it should then be added. Yield: 2 to 2¼ cups.

Mrs. Levi Schwartz
Berne, IN

Taco Salad Dip

½ pound ground beef
1 (15½ ounce) can refried beans
1 (8 ounce) can tomato sauce
1 package taco seasoning
¼ cup finely chopped onion
¼ cup finely chopped pepper

Preheat oven to 400 degrees. In a frying pan, brown ground beef thoroughly and drain. Stir in beans, tomato sauce, seasoning, onion, and pepper. Spread mixture in 9-inch pie plate. Heat mixture in oven for 10 minutes or until heated through.

Topping:
½ cup sour cream
1 tablespoon shredded cheese
⅛ teaspoon chili powder
1 cup chopped lettuce
1 cup shredded cheese

Mix sour cream, shredded cheese, and chili powder in a bowl and spread over beef mixture. Sprinkle with lettuce and shredded cheese. Serve with corn chips or crackers.

Vonda Yoder
Middlebury, IN

Chili-Corn Dip

1 (15 ounce) can corn, drained
1 (4 ounce) can chopped green chilies, undrained
1 cup sour cream
½ cup ranch dressing
4 teaspoons dry ranch dressing or dip powder
1 teaspoon black pepper
½ teaspoon garlic powder
¾ cup fried and crumbled bacon pieces
1 cup shredded cheddar cheese
Scoop-style corn chips or club crackers

In a mixing bowl, combine corn, chilies, sour cream, dressing, dry ranch powder, black pepper, and garlic powder together; then add bacon and cheese. Additional cheese and bacon pieces may be added. Refrigerate. Serve with corn chips or crackers.

Mary Miller
Shipshewana, IN

CREAMY CUCUMBER DIP

1 (8 ounce) package cream cheese, softened
1 cup sour cream
2 tablespoons salad dressing or mayonnaise
½ teaspoon Worcestershire sauce
1 medium cucumber, chopped
¼ cup chopped green pepper
1 round tablespoon chopped onion

In a mixing bowl, stir together cream cheese, sour cream, salad dressing, and Worcestershire sauce. Add cucumber, green pepper, and onion. Refrigerate for two hours before serving. Serve with your favorite crackers.

VONDA YODER
Middlebury, IN

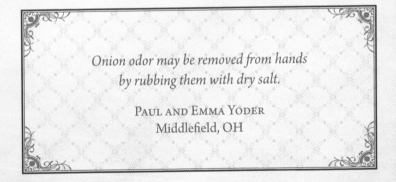

Onion odor may be removed from hands by rubbing them with dry salt.

PAUL AND EMMA YODER
Middlefield, OH

MUSTARD PRETZEL DIP

1 cup sour cream
1 cup mayonnaise
½ cup mustard
½ cup white sugar
2 tablespoons onion powder
1 package powdered Hidden Valley Ranch Dressing

Combine all ingredients together in a bowl and mix well. Serve with pretzels.

DANIEL AND LYDIA MILLER
Loudonville, OH

FRUIT DIP

1 (8 ounce) package cream cheese
1½ cup powdered sugar
1 cup sour cream
1 teaspoon lemon juice
1 large (16 ounce) tub whipped topping

Mix cream cheese, powdered sugar, sour cream, and lemon juice together. Add whipped topping. Serve as a dip to eat with fresh fruit—apples, pineapple, and grapes.

"Good as an afternoon snack on Christmas get-togethers."

MARY ALICE YODER
Topeka, IN

CHOCOLATE-CHIP CHEESE BALL

1 (8 ounce) package cream cheese
½ cup butter
¼ teaspoon vanilla
¾ cup powdered sugar
2 tablespoons brown sugar
1 (10½ ounce) package mini chocolate chips
¾ cup finely chopped nuts

Beat cream cheese, butter, and vanilla until fluffy in a mixing bowl. Gradually add sugars until combined. Stir in chips. Cover and refrigerate for 30 minutes. Place on large piece of plastic wrap and shape into a ball. Refrigerate at least one hour before serving. Roll ball in nuts. Serve with graham crackers.

BETTY MILLER
Middlefield, OH

OVEN CARAMEL CORN

1 cup packed brown sugar
½ cup butter
¼ cup light corn syrup
½ teaspoons salt
1 teaspoon baking soda
15 cups popped popcorn

Preheat oven to 200 degrees. Heat brown sugar, butter, syrup, and salt in saucepan until it comes to a boil. Simmer over medium-high heat, stirring for five minutes. Remove from heat. Stir in soda. Pour over popcorn and stir till well coated. Pour in two ungreased 9x13-inch pans. Bake for one hour, stirring every fifteen minutes.

1½ cup nuts may be added, but then popcorn should be decreased to 12 cups.

IVA YODER
Goshen, IN

HONEY MUSTARD PRETZELS

7 tablespoons honey mustard powder (available in bulk food stores)
¾ cup vegetable oil
1½ pound pretzel sticks

Preheat oven to 300 degrees. Mix powder and oil together in a bowl, and pour over pretzel sticks, stirring to coat. Bake on ungreased cookie sheet for one hour, stirring a couple of times during baking.

PAUL AND EMMA YODER
Middlefield, OH

Toasted Party Mix (Not So Salty)

¾ cup butter
¼ teaspoon onion powder
½ teaspoon Worcestershire sauce
¼ teaspoon celery salt
¼ teaspoon garlic salt
3 cups Cheerios cereal
3 cups Wheat Chex cereal
3 cups Rice Chex cereal
3 cups Corn Chex cereal
2 cups pretzel sticks
1½ cups mixed nuts

Preheat oven to 200 degrees. In a kettle, combine butter, onion powder, sauce, celery salt, and garlic salt over heat until butter is melted. Pour butter mixture over cereals and nuts, and then stir until coated. Bake uncovered on cookie sheets for one hour. Stir several times.

MARY AND KATIE YODER
Goshen, IN

Sweet and Salty Snack Mix

1 (11 ounce) bag pretzels
1 (10 ounce) package miniature cheese-filled crackers
1 cup dry roasted peanuts
1 cup white sugar
½ cup butter
½ cup light corn syrup
2 tablespoons vanilla
1 teaspoon baking soda
1 (10 ounce) bag M&M's
1 (18½ ounce) package candy corn

Preheat oven to 250 degrees. In a large bowl, combine pretzels, crackers, and peanuts. In a large saucepan, combine sugar, butter, and corn syrup. Bring to a boil over medium heat; boil for five minutes. Remove from heat; stir in vanilla and baking soda. (Mixture will foam). Pour over pretzel mixture and stir until coated. Pour into a greased 10x15x1-inch baking pan. Bake for 45 minutes, stirring every 10 to 15 minutes. Break apart while warm. Toss with M&M's and candy corn. Cool completely. Store mix in air-tight containers. Yield: 16 cups.

Doretta Yoder
Topeka, IN

CHRISTMAS PROGRAM

Shortly before Christmas, many Amish one-room schools have a special program, and every child takes part. Family members are invited to attend, as well as close friends and neighbors. In addition to wooden benches, school desks are used for seating.

For many days preceding the program, the children practice for the program so that everyone will know his or her lines before the big day. Simple decorations like snowflakes, stars, and Bethlehem scenes are made by the children, which makes the schoolhouse look quite festive.

The school's Christmas program is an exciting, joyous occasion where the children will sing songs, recite poems, or take part in short skits. All the songs are sung without any musical instruments to accompany them. Many of the songs, like "Silent Night" and "Joy to the World," are as familiar to the Amish as they are to the "English." Sometimes those in attendance are invited to sing along with the children. Although most of the program and many of the songs are performed in English, a few of the songs are sung in German.

During the program, the front of the room is often curtained off and simple props are used for the skits that are performed by the children. Some of the poems and skits are humorous, while others are of a more serious nature, depicting the true reason for the season. All recitations and songs are memorized.

The audience responds enthusiastically to each of the scholars performing in the program, and afterward, refreshments are usually served. When the evening is over, everyone returns home, happily filled with the wonder and genuine meaning of Christmas.

CHRISTMAS TRADITIONS

Amish families have their own special Christmas traditions, some of which they have been doing for many years. Here are a few examples:

On one of the days that the Yoder family from Topeka, Indiana, gets together during the holidays, the older folks sit down and enjoy the meal family style, while the children eat cafeteria-style. Once the table has been cleared, songbooks are passed out and everyone sings for a while. Following that, while some play games, a smorgasbord of snacks, candy, and drinks is enjoyed by all.

A tradition on Christmas Eve for the Miller family from Humboldt, Illinois, is to eat dinner by candlelight. Afterward, they have snacks and open their presents, also by candlelight. After the mess is cleaned up, the Millers play games. Each year, they usually get a new game to play on Christmas Eve.

The Knepp family, from Chouteau, Oklahoma, enjoys sledding on Christmas Day, if they have enough snow. They also have fun playing games, eating all the delicious food, and when possible, traveling to Indiana to visit their family.

One tradition that the Schwartz family from Berne, Indiana, enjoys is gathering their large family together for a big meal, followed by guessing games and lots of singing. Mrs. Schwartz furnishes all the warm food, and the desserts are brought in by their guests.

After a meal of soup, salad, or sandwiches on Christmas Eve, the Yoder family from Middlebury, Indiana, have their gift exchange. Then they play ping-pong and enjoy snacks of chips, dips, and candy throughout the evening.

No matter what tradition each Amish family has, they have one thing in common with other Amish church members—their emphasis at Christmas is on the birth of Jesus Christ.

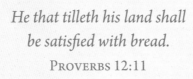

> *He that tilleth his land shall*
> *be satisfied with bread.*
>
> PROVERBS 12:11

Breads and Rolls

We don't need more to be thankful for;
we just need to be more thankful.

Cinnamon Rolls

1 cup milk
2 packages or 2 tablespoons yeast
1 cup warm water
2 eggs
½ cup butter, melted
⅔ cup sugar

1½ teaspoon salt
7 cups flour
4 tablespoons butter, melted
¾ cup brown sugar
3 teaspoons cinnamon

In a saucepan, scald the milk and cool slightly. Dissolve yeast in warm water. In a small bowl, beat eggs, melted butter, sugar, and salt. In a large bowl, combine milk with yeast mixture; then add the egg mixture and beat with a beater. Add 3 cups flour and beat again. Take a spoon and mix the remaining 4 cups of flour in. Cover and let rise in a warm place until doubled. Place raised dough on a floured surface and roll out ½-inch thick into a rectangle shape. Brush with melted butter. Mix brown sugar and cinnamon together, and sprinkle over the buttered dough. Roll up jelly-roll style starting with the long end and cut into 1-inch slices. Place slices cut side down in two greased 9x13-inch pans. Let rise till doubled.

Preheat oven to 350 degrees. Bake for 20 minutes. When cool, frost.

Frosting:

¼ cup sugar
¼ cup water
½ cup shortening

½ cup butter
1 egg
8 cups powdered sugar

In a saucepan, heat the sugar and water until syrupy (boil for 2 minutes). Mix shortening, butter, and egg together in a bowl, and then stir into the hot sugar water until well combined. Add powdered sugar and mix well.

Iva Yoder
Goshen, IN

Pumpkin Cinnamon Rolls

⅔ cup milk
4 tablespoons butter
1 cup pumpkin
4 tablespoons white sugar
1 teaspoon salt
2 eggs
2 packages or 2 tablespoons yeast
4 cups bread flour
2 tablespoons butter, melted
½ cup brown sugar
2 teaspoons cinnamon

In a small saucepan, heat milk and 4 tablespoons butter until warm (110 to 115 degrees). In a large bowl, combine the pumpkin, sugar, and salt. Add milk mixture. Beat in eggs and yeast. Add flour and mix well. Cover and let rise until doubled. Turn out raised dough on floured surface and knead until smooth. Roll out into a rectangle shape ½-inch thick. Brush on melted butter. Mix brown sugar and cinnamon together and sprinkle over the buttered dough. Roll up jelly-roll style starting with the long end. Slice into 1-inch slices. Place cut side down on lightly greased cookie sheet or in round pans with slices almost touching. Let rise in a warm place until doubled.

Preheat oven to 350 degrees. Bake for 20 minutes. Frost if desired.

Mary Rose Yoder
Shipshewana, IN

BACON CHEESE MUFFINS

2 cups flour
1 cup shredded cheddar cheese
8 bacon strips, fried and crumbled
2 tablespoons sugar
½ teaspoon garlic powder
3 teaspoons baking powder
¼ teaspoon salt
1 egg
1 cup milk
¼ cup vegetable oil

Preheat oven to 400 degrees. In a large bowl, combine flour, cheese, bacon, sugar, garlic, baking powder, and salt. In another bowl, beat the egg, milk, and oil. Stir liquid mixture into the dry ingredients just until moistened. Fill greased muffin pans ⅔ full. Bake for 15 to 20 minutes, or until toothpick comes out clean. Cool for 5 minutes before removing from pan. Yield: 1 dozen.

MARY ROSE YODER
Shipshewana, IN

Donut Muffins

1¾ cup flour
1½ teaspoons baking powder
½ teaspoon salt
½ teaspoon nutmeg
¼ teaspoon cinnamon
⅓ cup oil
¾ cup sugar
1 egg
¾ cup milk

TOPPING:
½ cup butter, melted
¾ cup sugar
1 teaspoon cinnamon

Preheat oven to 350 degrees. In a bowl, combine flour, baking powder, salt, nutmeg, and cinnamon. In another bowl, thoroughly combine oil, sugar, egg, and milk. Add liquid ingredients to dry ingredients, and stir together. Put in greased muffin pans, filling ⅔ full. Bake for 20 to 25 minutes. Shake muffins out immediately. While still hot, do the topping by dipping in melted butter and then in sugar and cinnamon combined. Optional: May use Christmas-colored sugars.

ARLENE WENGERD
Middlefield, OH

Kalochis

2 cups milk
1 cup butter
¼ cup sugar
2 teaspoons salt
2 tablespoons yeast
¼ cup warm water
6 egg yolks
6 cups flour
4 tablespoons butter, melted
1 (21 ounce) can fruit pie filling of your choice

In a saucepan, scald the milk and add butter, sugar, and salt. Let cool to lukewarm. Dissolve yeast in ¼ cup warm water and combine with the milk mixture along with the egg yolks. Add flour and mix well. Cover with cloth and let rise until doubled. Roll out 2 circles of dough ½-inch thick. Cut out with a round cookie cutter and put on ungreased cookie sheets. Brush with melted butter. Let rise until doubled again. Make indention in middle and fill with any kind of fruit filling. Let rise again until doubled. Preheat oven to 350 degrees. Bake for 15 minutes. When cool, they can be frosted.

Frosting:
8 tablespoons butter, melted
3 cups powdered sugar
1 teaspoon vanilla

In a bowl, mix together ingredients until blended. If needed, add a little hot water to make it spread nicely.

Linda Miller
Humboldt, IL

Buttery Corn Bread

¾ cup butter
1 cup sugar
3 eggs
1⅔ cup milk
1¾ cup flour
1 cup cornmeal
4½ teaspoons baking powder
1 teaspoon salt

Preheat oven to 400 degrees. In a mixing bowl, cream butter and sugar. Mix eggs and milk together. Combine the flour, cornmeal, baking powder, and salt together. Now add egg and dry ingredients alternately to the first mixture. Pour into greased 9x13-inch pan. Bake for 22 to 27 minutes or till done. It is very good with soup.

Sharon Knepp
Chouteau, OK

Pumpkin Cheese Bread

2½ cups sugar
½ cup margarine or butter
1 (8 ounce) package cream cheese
4 eggs
1 (16 ounce) can pumpkin
2 teaspoons baking soda
1 teaspoon cinnamon
¼ teaspoon ground cloves
3½ cups flour
1 teaspoon salt
½ teaspoon baking powder
1 cup chopped nuts

Preheat oven to 350 degrees. In a mixing bowl, combine sugar, margarine, and cream cheese, mixing at medium speed until well blended. Add eggs, one at a time, mixing well after each one. Blend in pumpkin. In a medium bowl, combine baking soda, cinnamon, cloves, flour, salt, and baking powder. Add dry mixture to wet mixture, mixing just until moistened. Fold in the nuts. Pour into two greased and floured 9x5-inch loaf pans. Bake for 1 hour or until it tests done. Cool 5 minutes and remove from pans.

RACHEL YODER
Burton, OH

QUICK STICKY BUNS

1¼ cups milk
¼ cup butter
3¼ cups flour, divided
¼ cup white sugar
1 teaspoon salt
2 tablespoons yeast
1 egg

In a saucepan, heat the milk and butter until very warm but not boiling. In a large bowl, combine the heated liquid with 2 cups flour, sugar, salt, yeast, and egg. Beat 4 minutes. Stir in the remaining flour. Cover and let rise for 30 minutes.

TOPPING:
1 cup brown sugar
2 tablespoons corn syrup
1 teaspoon cinnamon
½ cup butter
¾ cup nuts (chopped or whole)

In a small saucepan, heat the topping ingredients until sugar is dissolved.

Stir down the flour batter and drop by tablespoons in a greased 9x13-inch pan and pour the warm topping over the dough. Cover and let rise for 20 minutes. Preheat oven to 375 degrees and bake for 15 minutes.

IRENE MILLER
Shipshewana, IN

Swiss Buns (or Rolls)

2 cups milk
1 cup butter
½ cup white sugar
1 tablespoon salt
2 packages or 2 tablespoons yeast
¼ cup warm water
1 teaspoon white sugar
3 eggs, beaten
6½ cups flour
4 tablespoons melted butter
¾ cup brown sugar
3 teaspoons cinnamon

Preheat oven to 300 degrees. In a saucepan, scald the milk; add butter, sugar, and salt to melt. Put yeast in ¼ cup warm water and 1 teaspoon sugar till dissolved. Be sure to cool milk mixture to lukewarm before adding well-beaten eggs and yeast. Add flour until well mixed. Cover and let set till double in bulk, about an hour. On a floured surface, roll dough into a rectangle shape ½-inch thick and brush with melted butter and sprinkle with brown sugar and cinnamon. Roll up dough the long way and cut in 1-inch slices. In two greased 9x13-inch pans, place rolls cut side down; let rise again, about 30 minutes, and bake for 35 minutes or until done.

Barbara Troyer
Millersburg, OH

FLUFFY BISCUITS

2 cups flour
4 teaspoons baking powder
2 teaspoons sugar
½ teaspoon salt
½ teaspoon cream of tartar
½ cup shortening
⅔ cup milk

Preheat oven to 450 degrees. In a large bowl, sift flour, baking powder, sugar, salt, and cream of tartar together. Cut in shortening until mixture resembles coarse crumbs. Add milk all at once and stir just till dough follows the fork around the bowl. Roll out to ½-inch thick and cut with biscuit cutter or round cookie cutter. Place on ungreased cookie sheet. Bake for 10 to 12 minutes.

MARY K. BONTRAGER
Middlebury, IN

CRESCENT OVERNIGHT DINNER ROLLS

1 package or 1 tablespoon yeast
1 tablespoon sugar
1 cup warm water
3 eggs
½ cup sugar
½ cup shortening
½ teaspoon salt
5 cups flour
4 tablespoons butter, melted

In a large bowl, mix together the yeast and 1 tablespoon sugar. Add warm water and eggs and beat together. Add sugar, shortening, salt, and flour. Stir until combined. Knead dough well. Cover dough tightly with cloth and refrigerate overnight.

Divide dough in 2 parts and roll out in 12-inch circles. Cut each circle into 16 wedges. Roll up starting with wide side. Place on ungreased cookie sheet, cover, and let rise 3 to 4 hours.

Preheat oven to 400 degrees and bake for 15 minutes. Brush with butter and serve while warm. Yield: 32 rolls.

MRS. LEVI SCHWARTZ
Berne, IN

DINNER ROLLS

1 tablespoon yeast
1 tablespoon sugar
½ cup warm water
½ cup vegetable oil
1 cup warm water
⅓ cup sugar
1¼ teaspoon salt
4½ cups flour, divided

In a bowl, mix the yeast, 1 tablespoon sugar, and ½ cup warm water together and let set for 5 to 10 minutes. In a large bowl, mix oil, 1 cup water, ⅓ cup sugar, and salt together. Add the dissolved yeast mixture until combined. Add 2½ cups of flour and stir well. Add the remaining 2 cups flour and mix well. Knead for 5 to 7 minutes. Cover and let rise for 1 hour or until double in size. Punch down, let rise another 30 minutes. Butter two 9-inch pans. Divide dough in half and shape into 12 rolls per pan or butter 2 bread pans and make two 1-pound loaves. Cover and let rise till double in size. Preheat oven to 325 degrees. Bake for 25 to 30 minutes. Yield: 24 rolls or 2 loaves of bread.

IVA YODER
Goshen, IN

Homemade Bread

3 tablespoons yeast
3 cups water, divided
4 tablespoons shortening
⅔ cup sugar
1½ tablespoon salt
6 cups flour

In a bowl, dissolve yeast in 1 cup lukewarm water. Pour 2 cups boiling water in a large bowl and add shortening, sugar, and salt. Let cool to lukewarm. Stir in dissolved yeast. Add flour and stir until dough is smooth. Cover and let rise till double in size in a warm place. Knead down well (5 to 7 minutes) and let rise 2 more times. Put into 3 greased bread pans and let rise again. Preheat oven to 375 degrees. Bake for 30 minutes or until golden brown. Yield: 3 loaves.

Amanda Schwartz
Monroe, IN

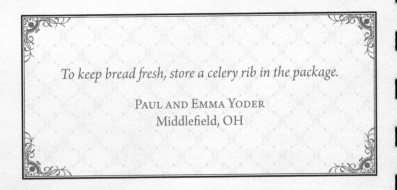

To keep bread fresh, store a celery rib in the package.

Paul and Emma Yoder
Middlefield, OH

PIZZA BREAD

1 tablespoon yeast
1 cup warm water
1 teaspoon sugar
2 tablespoons olive oil
1 teaspoon salt
2½ cups flour
2 eggs, divided and beaten
1 teaspoon Italian seasoning, divided
1 teaspoon seasoned salt, divided
4 ounces shaved ham
4 ounces sliced pepperoni
1 cup shredded cheese

Preheat oven to 350 degrees. In a mixing bowl, dissolve yeast in warm water. Add sugar, oil, salt, and flour and mix until combined. Cover with cloth and let rise until doubled. Roll out on a floured cookie sheet. Beat an egg and spread it over the dough. Sprinkle with half of Italian seasoning and half of seasoned salt. Put slices of ham and pepperoni in the center of the dough and spread cheese over all. Fold in the sides of the pizza covering the meats and cheese. Spread another beaten egg over the top and sprinkle the remaining seasonings on top. Bake for 20 minutes.

LOVINA MILLER
Shipshewana, IN

CHRISTMAS MEALS

A traditional Amish Christmas dinner is one of the highlights of the family Christmas celebration. The meal is similar to what most "English" people serve their families on Christmas Day. It might include roast turkey or chicken, along with stuffing, potatoes, gravy, one or more kinds of cooked vegetables, salads, pickles, homemade relish, rolls or bread, and cranberries. For dessert, there may be cookies, candy, cake, or several kinds of pies.

After the big meal, many Amish families sing Christmas carols. Following that, the adults sit and visit or play ping-pong or board games. The young people will often go outside for some type of game, like volleyball, while the younger children

play in the house or outside in the yard. Throughout the afternoon and evening, everyone eats some of the leftovers from the earlier meal, as well as dips, salty snacks, candy, and cookies, along with coffee and other refreshing beverages.

Since the Amish have extended families, many of their Christmas gatherings and holiday meals extend well into the months of January and February. In addition to the family gatherings, there are often dinners for groups of friends, get-togethers for teachers, and gatherings for single women. As one Amish friend said, "Coming together, seeing everyone happy and eating all the goodies we don't make except for Christmas, is one of the things I like best about the holiday."

CHRISTMAS GIFTS

The ministers in the Amish church encourage their members to focus on Christ's coming to earth and not on worldly things. However, part of most Amish Christmas celebrations includes giving gifts to family members and, sometimes, close friends. Some Amish families draw names and are only required to give one Christmas gift to the person whose name they drew. Others may give a gift to each family member.

Some of the gifts are store-bought, but many are homemade. An Amish child might receive a toy, books, game, puzzle, bicycle, clothes, or even a new pony. Older Amish girls may get something they can put in their hope chest, such as dishes, quilts, or house wares. Older Amish boys sometimes

receive tools, a hunting rifle, or something they may need for their horse.

Some Amish schoolchildren will give a small gift to their teacher, and after drawing a name, they often trade gifts with a fellow classmate. Dating couples also exchange gifts at Christmas, and if the couple is considering marriage, the young man might give his girlfriend a set of china dishes, silverware, or something useful like a clock.

Before the gifts are handed out on Christmas Eve or Christmas morning, the family will usually gather for devotions and the reading of the Gospel account of the birth of Christ. Amish parents want their children to understand the true meaning of Christmas and that the gifts they receive are not from a fictional Santa Claus, but from their parents.

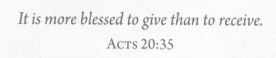

It is more blessed to give than to receive.

ACTS 20:35

Gifts from the Kitchen

We make a living by what we get;
we make a life by what we give.

TRASH (CHRISTMAS SNACK)

2 pounds (32 ounces) white chocolate coating
¼ cup butterscotch chips
1 (16 ounce) bag pretzels
5 cups Cheerios cereal
1 (12.6 ounce) bag M&M's
1 (16 ounce) jar peanuts

In a saucepan, carefully melt the white chocolate and butterscotch chips together. Put the pretzels, Cheerios, M&M's, and peanuts in a large bowl. Pour melted coating over the ingredients in the bowl and stir gently. Pour on wax paper and spread out evenly. When cool, break into pieces and store in an airtight container.

LUCY GRABER
Bloomfield, IA

SILLY PUTTY

◇◇

2 cups Elmer's glue
1½ cups hot water
4 tablespoons 20 Mule Team Borax
½ cup water

In a bowl, combine glue and hot water together. In a different bowl,
dissolve borax in ½ cup warm water. Combine ingredients from
both bowls into one, mixing with your hands until it forms a ball.
Store putty in an airtight container.

"Kids have fun playing with this!"

VONDA YODER
Middlebury, IN

Cappuccino Mix in a Jar

4 cups powdered coffee creamer
2 cups dry powdered milk
3 tablespoons Nestle Quik chocolate powder
¾ cup instant coffee
1½ cups powdered sugar
½ teaspoon salt

Place ingredients in a bowl and mix well. Put into a quart jar for gift giving or store in airtight container for personal use. Use ¼ cup of the mix to 1 cup hot water to make a tasty drink.

LINDA MILLER
Humboldt, IL

Hot Chocolate Mix in a Jar

1 (8 quart) box of dry instant milk
2 pounds (32 ounce) of powdered sugar
1 (12 ounce) jar powdered coffee creamer
2 pounds (32 ounce) Nestle Quik chocolate powder

In a bowl, mix together the ingredients and put in a quart jar for gift giving or store in airtight container for personal use. Use ⅓ cup mix to 1 cup hot water for each drink.

MRS. LEVI SCHWARTZ
Berne, IN

COOKIE MIX IN A JAR

◇◇

¼ cup white sugar
⅝ cup oats
¼ teaspoon salt
¼ cup brown sugar
⅞ cup flour
1 cup chocolate chips
⅝ cup oats
¼ cup brown sugar
⅓ cup each walnuts, M&Ms, coconut

Layer ingredients in order given into a wide mouth jar. Put lid on and attach the following instructions for baking:

Preheat oven to 375 degrees. Combine together ½ cup softened butter, 1 egg, ½ teaspoon baking soda, 1 tablespoon milk, and 1 tablespoon vanilla. Add the mix from the jar, mix well. Drop by teaspoons on a cookie sheet. Bake for 10 minutes.

RACHEL YODER
Burton, OH

Brownies in a Jar

1¼ cups flour
8 tablespoons cocoa
½ cup brown sugar, packed
1½ cups white sugar
1 teaspoon salt
½ cup chopped walnuts (optional)

Layer ingredients in order into a wide mouth quart jar. Cover with a lid and decorate to give as a gift. Attach the following instructions to the jar:

Preheat oven to 350 degrees. In a bowl, mix together ½ cup melted butter, 3 beaten eggs, and 1 teaspoon vanilla; then add contents of the jar. Stir until combined. Spread into a greased 8x8-inch pan, and bake for 40 to 45 minutes or until done.

Betty Bricker
Middlefield, OH

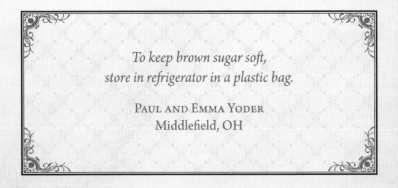

To keep brown sugar soft,
store in refrigerator in a plastic bag.

Paul and Emma Yoder
Middlefield, OH

CRUNCHY PEANUT BUTTER BALLS

1 cup peanut butter
1 (7 ounce) jar marshmallow crème
1½ cup Rice Krispies cereal
1 (12 ounce) package chocolate chips, melted

In a bowl, mix together the peanut butter, marshmallow crème, and Rice Krispies; form into balls. Chill. Dip in melted chocolate. Store or give as a gift in a container with a lid.

SALOMA YODER
Middlefield, OH

PEANUT CLUSTERS

1 pound (16 ounces) salted peanuts
2 pounds (32 ounce) milk chocolate

Have peanuts at room temperature. Melt chocolate slowly over medium-low heat. Add peanuts and drop on wax paper by teaspoon full. Chill until hardened, then store in a container with a lid.

MRS. LEVI SCHWARTZ
Berne, IN

Christmas Hard Candy

3¾ cups sugar
1½ cup light corn syrup
1 cup water
2 to 3 drops red food coloring or color of your choice
¼ teaspoon watermelon flavoring or flavoring of your choice
½ cup powdered sugar

Butter two 15x10x1-inch pans and set aside. In a large heavy saucepan, combine sugar, corn syrup, water, and food coloring. Cook and stir over medium heat until sugar is dissolved. Bring to a boil. Cook, without stirring, until candy thermometer reads 300 degrees (hard-crack stage). Remove from heat; stir in flavoring. Pour into pans; cool. Dust with powdered sugar; break into pieces. Store the candy in airtight containers. Yield: 2 pounds.

Saloma Yoder
Middlefield, OH

PEANUT BUTTER FUDGE

◇◇

2 cups sugar
½ cup milk
1⅓ cup peanut butter
1 (7 ounce) jar marshmallow crème

In a saucepan, bring sugar and milk to a boil; boil 3 minutes. Add peanut butter and marshmallow crème. Mix well. Quickly pour into a buttered loaf pan. Chill until set. Cut into squares and store in a container with a lid.

LEONA MULLET
Burton, OH

LAYERED MINT CHOCOLATE FUDGE

12 ounces chocolate coating wafers
1 (14 ounce) can sweetened condensed milk, divided
2 teaspoons vanilla
1 cup white chocolate coating wafers
1 tablespoon peppermint extract or a few drops peppermint oil
1 drop green food coloring (optional)

In a saucepan, over low heat, melt chocolate wafers with 1 cup condensed milk; add vanilla. Spread half of mixture into 8 or 9-inch square pan lined with wax paper. Chill 10 minutes or until firm. Hold remaining chocolate mixture at room temperature. Over low heat, melt white chocolate wafers with remaining condensed milk; add peppermint extract and food coloring. Spread on chilled chocolate layer. Chill 10 minutes or until firm. Spread reserved chocolate mixture on mint layer. Chill 2 hours or until firm. Cut in squares and store in air-tight container. Yield: 1¾ pounds.

BETTY MILLER
Middlefield, OH

MILK CHOCOLATE FUDGE

¾ cup margarine or butter
3 cups sugar
⅔ cup evaporated milk
1 (12 ounce) package milk chocolate or vanilla chips
1 (7 ounce) jar marshmallow crème
1 teaspoon vanilla
1 cup chopped walnuts (optional)

Combine margarine, sugar, and milk in heavy saucepan. Bring to full boil, stirring constantly. Continue boiling for 5 minutes over medium heat or until candy thermometer reaches 234 degrees. Remove from heat. Gradually stir in chips until melted. Add marshmallow crème and vanilla. Mix well. Walnuts can be added. Pour into a buttered 9x9-inch pan. Cool at room temperature and store in a container with a lid.

KATHRYN YODER
Burton, OH

Never Fail Caramels

1 (14 ounce) can sweetened condensed milk
2 cups sugar
2 cups light corn syrup
1 cup butter
2 tablespoons vanilla

Combine all ingredients, except the vanilla, in a saucepan. Cook slowly to 250 degrees. Mixture should boil very slowly. It must be stirred constantly. Remove from heat and add vanilla. Pour in a buttered sheet cake pan. Let cool till set and store in container with a lid.

Linda Miller
Humboldt, IL

VALLEY TAFFY

1 package unflavored Knox gelatin
¼ cup cold water
2 cups white sugar
2 cups light corn syrup
2 cups heavy cream
Paraffin, the size of a walnut

Put gelatin in cold water to dissolve. In a heavy sauce pan, put the sugar, syrup, cream, and paraffin and bring to a boil for 15 minutes. Then add the gelatin water and continue boiling until a hard ball forms in cold water (252 degrees). Pour in greased pie pans and cool until it can be handled. Have 2 people pull it until it gets nice and light colored. Pull it into long strings and place them on a buttered counter top or hard surface till cooled. Cut into bite size pieces and store in a container with a lid.

LYDIA MILLER
Goshen, IN

Gumdrops

4 packages unflavored Knox gelatin
2 cups water, divided
3 cups sugar
1 package Kool-Aid drink mix, any flavor
1 tablespoon lemon juice
1 cup fine white sugar

In a small bowl, put the gelatin in 1 cup water to dissolve. In a kettle, bring 1 cup water and sugar to a boil. Add softened gelatin. Boil for 30 minutes. Remove from heat and add 1 package of Kool-Aid and lemon juice. Pour into a greased 9x13-inch pan; cool quickly. Cut into small squares and roll in fine white sugar. Store in a container with a lid.

Saloma Yoder
Middlefield, OH

GRANDMA'S DIVINITY

3 cups sugar
⅔ cup water
½ cup light corn syrup
2 egg whites
1 teaspoon vanilla
1 cup chopped pecans

Line three 15x10x1-inch pans with wax paper. In a large heavy saucepan, combine the sugar, water, and corn syrup; bring to a boil, stirring constantly to dissolve sugar. Cook, without stirring, over medium heat until a candy thermometer reads 252 degrees (hard-ball stage). Just before the temperature is reached, in a separate bowl, beat the egg whites until stiff peaks form. Slowly add hot sugar mixture in a thin stream over egg whites, beating constantly and scraping sides of bowl occasionally. Add vanilla. Beat until candy holds its shape, about 5 to 6 minutes. (Do not over mix or candy will get stiff and crumbly.) Immediately fold in pecans. Quickly drop by heaping teaspoonful onto prepared pans. Let stand until dry. Store the candy between wax paper in an air-tight container at room temperature.

SALOMA YODER
Middlefield, OH

Rocky Road Fudge Bars

½ cup butter
1 (1 ounce) square baking
   chocolate
1 cup sugar

1 cup flour
1 teaspoon baking powder
2 eggs

Preheat oven to 350 degrees. In a saucepan melt butter and chocolate. Add sugar, flour, baking powder, and eggs, mixing well. Spread into greased 9x13-inch pan.

Filling:

6 ounces cream cheese
2 tablespoons flour
¼ cup butter

1 egg
6 ounces chocolate chips
2 cups miniature marshmallows

In a bowl, combine cream cheese, flour, butter, an egg, and fold in chocolate chips. Spread over bar mixture. Bake for 25 to 30 minutes. Take out of oven and immediately sprinkle with marshmallows.

Topping:

½ cup butter, softened
2 tablespoons cocoa
2 ounces cream cheese

¼ cup milk
1 pound powdered sugar

In a bowl, combine all topping ingredients together until smooth. Pour over marshmallows. Cut into bars when cool. Store in a container with a lid.

Lucy Graber
Bloomfield, IA

O Henry Bars

1 cup white sugar
1 cup light corn syrup
1½ cup peanut butter
6 cups Rice Krispies cereal
1 cup chocolate chips
1 cup butterscotch chips

In a kettle, bring sugar and corn syrup to a slight boil. Remove from heat, add peanut butter, and stir until smooth. Stir in Rice Krispies and mix well. Pat into buttered 9x13-inch pan. Melt chips over low heat and spread over the cereal mixture like frosting. When cool, cut into bars and store in a container with a lid.

LEONA MULLET
Burton, OH

CHRISTMAS MUSIC

Music plays an important role in the Amish religion, and especially during the special time of Christmas celebrations. Most Amish families will pass out songbooks and gather together for a time of singing after their Christmas meal. Many of the songs they sing are traditional carols like "Silent Night" and "Star of Bethlehem," but sometimes "Jingle Bells" is sung for the benefit of the children. Other songs found in the Amish songbooks that aren't traditionally Christmas, such as "Light at the River," "Kneel at the Cross," and "Wonder of Love," are also sung. Some of the songs are sung in English and some in German.

During the weeks before Christmas, Amish young people will often climb aboard a horse-drawn wagon filled with bales of hay that have been covered with blankets. Then they head out for an evening of caroling around their neighborhood.

In addition to Christmas carols, they will frequently sing, "We Wish You a Merry Christmas" before leaving each home. Sometimes the word *Merry* is replaced with *Blessed*. The carolers will often go to someone's home afterward for a supper that might consist of soup, sandwiches, cake, and ice cream, or some other light meal.

At the school Christmas program, Amish children enjoy singing a variety of Christmas songs, and their family and friends are encouraged to sing along. All of the songs are sung without the use of any musical instruments, but the sound of so many voices blended together is a beautiful reminder of what Christmas is all about.

CHRISTMAS DECORATIONS AND CARDS

Christmas decorations in an Amish home, if there are any, are simple and focused on the religious meaning of the holiday. There are no Christmas trees in the house or colored twinkle lights adorning the outside of the home. Evergreen boughs and candles may decorate some Amish homes, as well as any Christmas cards they may have received from their "English" friends or neighbors.

If the Amish community practices the exchange of Christmas cards, they are usually sent to their non-Amish friends. Although some of the cards may be purchased, many of the Christmas greetings are homemade, using rubber stamps and colored pens or markers to create pretty scenes on the front, with a handwritten sentiment on the inside. Sometimes the edges of the cards are cut with scalloped-edge scissors to make them look more special. Some Amish families will hang the cards they receive around the living room in their home to be enjoyed during the holiday season.

In addition to the cards, friends or family members often get together to make gifts of cookies and candies that will be given to friends and neighbors, and even to some who aren't part of the Amish community. An Amish friend from Illinois bakes dozens of cookies and pies to give away during the Christmas season. Among the Amish, Christmas is a special time of giving and fellowshipping with others.

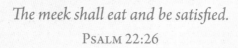

The meek shall eat and be satisfied.
PSALM 22:26

Salads, Main Dishes, and Sides

Our needs will never exhaust God's supply.

CHRISTMAS CRUNCH SALAD

4 cups broccoli
4 cups cauliflower
1 medium red onion, chopped
4 cherry tomatoes, halved

DRESSING:
1 cup mayonnaise
½ cup sour cream
1 to 2 tablespoons sugar
1 tablespoon vinegar
Salt and pepper to taste

Cut up vegetables and put in a bowl. In another bowl, combine dressing ingredients and pour over vegetables and toss. Cover and chill in refrigerator for 1 to 2 hours.

ARLENE WENGERD
Middlefield, OH

*For leftover salad, put a paper towel over
the top instead of a lid. This keeps the salad fresh,
and the cheese, if used in a salad, will not get soggy.*

VONDA YODER
Middlebury, IN

ORIENTAL CHICKEN SALAD

1 medium head lettuce, chopped
2 cups chopped grilled chicken breast
1 cup salted cashews
1 (8 ounce) can water chestnuts, sliced
2 cups chow mein noodles
1 small onion, chopped, or 1 tablespoon dried minced onion

In a large bowl, combine the salad ingredients together.

DRESSING:
½ cup ketchup
¾ cup sugar
¼ cup vinegar
½ cup vegetable oil
1 tablespoon Miracle Whip salad dressing
2 tablespoons minced dried onion
1 teaspoon salt

In another bowl, beat dressing ingredients together. Pour over salad and toss just before serving.

LOVINA MILLER
Shipshewana, IN

PASTA SALAD

16 ounces spiral pasta, cooked, rinsed, and drained
1 head cauliflower, cut fine
1 large bunch broccoli, cut fine
1 cup cheese cubes (optional)

In a large bowl, combine cooked pasta, cauliflower, broccoli, and cheese together.

DRESSING:
1 quart mayonnaise
1 package Italian dressing mix
1 package ranch dressing mix

Mix dressing ingredients together and pour over vegetables mixture. If needed, add a bit of sugar and salt. If too dry, add more mayonnaise.

BETTY BRICKER
Middlefield, OH

Ribbon Salad

◇◇

1 (6 ounce) box lime gelatin
5 cups boiling water, divided
4 cups cold water, divided
1 (3 ounce) box lemon gelatin
1 (8 ounce) package cream cheese
½ cup sugar
1 (16 ounce) container whipped topping
1 (6 ounce) box cherry gelatin

In a mixing bowl, dissolve lime gelatin in 2 cups of boiling water and then add 2 cups of cold water and pour into a 14x10x2-inch pan. Let set. In another bowl, dissolve lemon gelatin in 1 cup boiling water; let cool. Mix cream cheese with sugar in a separate bowl, stir in lemon gelatin, and add whipped topping. Spread onto lime gelatin. Let set. In a bowl, dissolve cherry gelatin in 2 cups of boiling water, add 2 cups of cold water, and cool until syrupy. Pour over cream cheese layer. Chill until firm.

RACHEL YODER
Burton, OH

CHILI CORN BREAD SALAD

1 (8½ ounce) box corn bread muffin mix
1 (7 ounce) can chopped green chilies, undrained
⅛ teaspoon ground cumin
⅛ teaspoon dried oregano
1 cup mayonnaise
1 cup sour cream
1 envelope Ranch salad dressing mix
2 (15 ounce) cans pinto beans, drained and rinsed
2 (15¼ ounce) cans whole kernel corn, drained
3 medium tomatoes, chopped
1 cup chopped green pepper
1 cup chopped green onion
10 bacon strips, fried and crumbled
2 cups shredded cheddar cheese

Preheat oven to 400 degrees. Prepare corn bread batter according to package directions. Stir in the chilies, cumin, and oregano. Spread into greased 8x8-inch pan. Bake for 20 to 25 minutes or until toothpick comes out clean. Cool.

In a small bowl, combine mayonnaise, sour cream, and dressing mix; set aside. Crumble half the cornbread into a 9x13-inch pan. Layer over the cornbread with half each of the beans, mayo mixture, corn, tomatoes, peppers, onions, bacon, and cheese. Repeat layers once, starting again with cornbread. Dish will be very full. Cover and refrigerate at least 2 hours before serving.

DORETTA YODER
Topeka, IN

CHEDDAR HAM CHOWDER

2 cups water
4 teaspoons powdered ham base
2 cups peeled and cubed potatoes
½ cup diced carrots
¼ cup chopped onion
½ cup sliced celery
1 (16 ounce) can kernel corn, drained
¼ teaspoon pepper
¼ cup butter
¼ cup flour
1 teaspoon garlic salt
2½ cups milk
2 to 3 cups shredded cheddar cheese
2 cups cubed ham
10 bacon strips, cooked and crumbled

Bring water and ham base to boil in soup pot. Add potatoes, carrots, onion, celery, corn, and pepper. Bring to a boil, reduce heat, and simmer for 8 to 10 minutes, or until vegetables are tender. Remove from heat. In a medium saucepan, melt the butter. Blend in flour and add garlic salt. Slowly add milk, stirring constantly. Cook until thickened. Add cheese; stir until melted. Stir cheese mixture into pot of vegetables. Return soup pot to heat. Add ham and bacon; heat through, stirring occasionally.

SALOMA YODER
Middlefield, OH

BAKED POTATO SOUP

⅔ cup margarine or butter
⅔ cup flour
7 cups milk
4 large potatoes, baked and chopped
¼ cup chopped onion
12 strips bacon, cooked and crumbled
1¼ cup shredded cheddar cheese
1 cup sour cream
¾ teaspoon salt
½ teaspoon pepper
1 tablespoon fresh or dried chives

In 4-quart kettle, melt the margarine and stir in flour till smooth. Add milk, stirring constantly, till thick. Add potatoes and onions. Bring to boil, stirring constantly. Reduce heat and let simmer for 10 minutes. Add the bacon, cheese, sour cream, salt, pepper, and chives. Stir until the cheese melts. Serve.

Sharon Knepp
Chouteau, OK

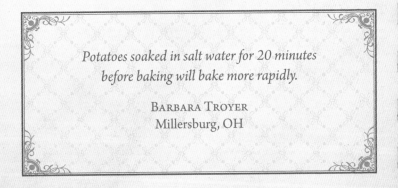

Potatoes soaked in salt water for 20 minutes before baking will bake more rapidly.

Barbara Troyer
Millersburg, OH

CHILI SOUP

1 pound hamburger
2 cups tomato juice
2 cups pizza sauce
2 cups water
1 cup pork and beans
⅓ cup brown sugar
1 teaspoon chili powder

In a soup pot, brown hamburger; drain excess grease. Then add tomato juice, pizza sauce, water, beans, brown sugar, and chili powder. Bring to a boil; then simmer until ready to eat. Best if simmered for 1 hour or more.

LOVINA MILLER
Shipshewana, IN

BROCCOLI CHEESE SOUP

½ cup butter
¾ cup flour
2 quarts (8 cups) milk
2 small bunches broccoli, cut up and cooked
2 cups cubed Velveeta processed cheese
1 teaspoon salt
¼ teaspoon pepper

In a saucepan, melt butter. Add flour and stir. Add milk, a little at a time, beating with wire whisk until smooth. Add cooked broccoli and bring to a boil on low heat, stirring occasionally. Add cheese, salt, and pepper and let stand until cheese is melted. Serve.

RACHEL YODER
Burton, OH

To cut down on odors when cooking cabbage, cauliflower, or broccoli, add a little vinegar to the water.

VONDA YODER
Middlebury, IN

Pizza Soup

1 pound sausage
¼ cup water
½ onion, chopped
½ green pepper, chopped
Season to taste with Italian seasoning, garlic powder, basil, rosemary,
   salt, and pepper
2 quarts (8 cups) pizza sauce
4 cups water
2 ounces pepperoni, chopped
½ cup shredded mozzarella cheese

Brown sausage in a skillet. Add ¼ cup water, onions, and peppers,
and sauté with sausage until tender. Add seasonings to taste. Put
pizza sauce and water in a large sauce pan. Add the sausage mixture
and pepperoni. Bring to boil and simmer for 15 minutes. When
serving, top each bowl of soup with shredded mozzarella. This is
very good with buttery cornbread.

Sharon Knepp
Chouteau, OK

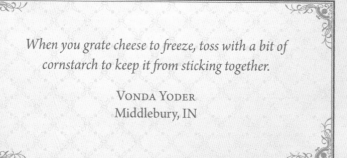

When you grate cheese to freeze, toss with a bit of
cornstarch to keep it from sticking together.

Vonda Yoder
Middlebury, IN

POTATO SOUP

2 large potatoes, grated
1 large onion, chopped
2 cloves garlic, minced
2 cups chicken broth
4 cups water
1 pound sausage, browned
½ cup crumbled bacon
Season to taste with salt, pepper, Italian seasonings, and parsley
1 cup heavy whipping cream
¼ cup fresh parsley leaves

Place potatoes, onion, garlic, broth, and water in a large pot and
cook until potatoes are done. Add browned sausage and bacon.
Add spices to taste. Simmer for 10 minutes more. Turn to low heat
and add cream. Heat through and serve. Garnish with fresh parsley
leaves.

DIANNA YODER
Goshen, IN

Wet Burritos

1½ pound hamburger
1 onion, diced
1 package taco seasoning
1 (16 ounce) can refried beans
1 (16 ounce) container sour cream
1 (10¾ ounce) can cream of mushroom soup
1 package (6 inch) soft tortilla shells
4 cups shredded yellow cheese
2 or 3 tomatoes, chopped
½ head lettuce, chopped

Preheat oven to 350 degrees. In a frying pan, brown hamburger and onions; drain grease. Add taco seasoning and beans. In a mixing bowl, mix the sour cream and soup together. Spread ½ of the sour cream and soup mixture on bottom of cookie sheet with sides. Fill shells with meat/bean mixture and roll up. Put in cookie sheet. Spread remaining sour cream/soup mixture on top of shells. Top with cheese. Bake for 15 minutes or till cheese melts and burritos are hot. Serve with lettuce and tomatoes on top.

Iva Yoder
Goshen, IN

TRUCKER BEANS

1 pound ground beef
1 small onion, chopped
1 (15 ounce) can pork and beans
1 (15 ounce) can lima beans, drained
1 (15 ounce) can kidney beans, drained
⅓ cup brown sugar
⅓ cup white sugar
¼ cup ketchup
¼ cup barbecue sauce
1 teaspoon mustard
¼ teaspoon chili powder

Preheat oven to 325 degrees. Brown beef and onion together in a large frying pan. Drain off excess grease. Add the beans, sugars, ketchup, barbecue sauce, mustard, and chili powder; combine. Put into a casserole dish. Bake for 1 hour. Note: Can also use green beans or other favorite beans.

ARLENE WENGERD
Middlefield, OH

Spicy Sandwich Loaf

1 tablespoon butter
1 cup sliced mushrooms
½ cup chopped green pepper
1 pound frozen bread dough, thawed
4 ounces ham, thinly sliced
4 ounces salami, thinly sliced
4 ounces shredded mozzarella cheese
1½ ounces pepperoni, thinly sliced

Melt butter in a large skillet. Add mushrooms and peppers; cook, stirring often until tender. Set aside. On a large baking sheet lined with aluminum foil, press dough into a 10x13-inch rectangle. Layer the ham, salami, cheese, and pepperoni down center of dough. Top with mushrooms and peppers. Fold sides of dough, overlapping the edges. Turn the seam side down and pinch ends together. Let rise for 1 hour. Preheat oven to 350 degrees. Bake for 30 to 40 minutes until golden brown. Good served hot or cold.

BETTY BRICKER
Middlefield, OH

Taco Pizza

2 cups flour
1 teaspoon salt
2 teaspoons baking powder
¼ cup cooking oil
⅔ cup milk

Preheat oven to 350 degrees. Mix flour, salt, baking powder, oil, and milk together in a bowl. Roll out on 14-inch pizza pan. Bake crust for 25 minutes.

Topping:
1½ pound ground beef, browned
1 (16 ounce) can refried beans
1 tablespoon taco seasoning
⅔ cup cream of mushroom soup
⅔ cup sour cream
2 cups shredded cheese
½ head lettuce, chopped
2 or 3 tomatoes, diced
1 bag of tortilla chips
1 (16 ounce) French Dressing

In a frying pan, brown meat; then add beans and taco seasoning. In a separate bowl, mix soup and sour cream. When crust is baked, spread sour cream mixture on crust. Put hamburger mixture on top of sour cream. Top with cheese. Return to oven until cheese is melted. When ready to serve, layer with lettuce, tomatoes, and broken chips and drizzle French dressing over all.

Lucy Graber
Bloomfield, IA

Honey Mustard Ham and Cheese Sandwiches

〰〰〰〰〰〰〰〰〰〰〰〰〰〰〰〰〰〰〰〰〰〰〰〰〰〰〰〰〰〰〰〰〰〰〰〰

1 dozen dinner rolls or mini sub buns
12 slices ham
12 slices of Swiss cheese

Prepare mini sandwiches and put in single layer onto cake pans.

TOPPING:
½ cup butter
2 tablespoons prepared mustard
2 tablespoons Worcestershire Sauce
⅓ cup brown sugar

Preheat oven to 325 degrees. In a saucepan, combine butter, mustard, sauce, and brown sugar together over heat until butter and sugar are melted; drizzle across tops of sandwiches. Bake uncovered for 25 minutes.

DORETTA YODER
Topeka, IN

Sweet and Sour Meatloaf

1½ pound ground beef
1 medium onion, chopped
1 cup saltine cracker crumbs
1 teaspoon pepper
1½ teaspoon salt
½ cup tomato paste
1 egg, beaten

Preheat oven to 350 degrees. In a mixing bowl, combine ground beef and onion. Add crumbs, pepper, salt, paste, and egg; mix well. Shape into loaf and place in a 9x5-inch loaf pan.

TOPPING:
½ cup tomato sauce
1 cup water
2 tablespoons vinegar
2 tablespoons mustard
2 tablespoons brown sugar

In a mixing bowl, combine sauce, water, vinegar, mustard, and brown sugar and spread over the meat. Bake for 1½ hours.

BARBARA TROYER
Millersburg, OH

Hot Wings

5 pounds frozen chicken wings
¾ cup butter
1 (16 ounce) bottle honey barbeque sauce
½ cup brown sugar
½ (5 ounce) bottle hot sauce

Preheat oven to 350 degrees. Place frozen chicken wings in 9x13-inch pan and bake for 1 hour. In a saucepan, melt butter and add barbeque sauce, sugar, and hot sauce; mix well. Pour over the baked wings. Return to the oven and bake at 300 degrees for another 45 minutes.

Variation: I like to use chicken tenders instead of chicken wings.

RACHEL YODER
Burton, OH

Cranberry Chicken

1 (16 ounce) bottle French dressing
1 package onion soup mix
1 (16 ounce) can whole berry cranberry sauce
2½ pounds chicken breast

Preheat oven to 350 degrees. In a bowl, mix dressing, soup mix, and sauce together and pour over chicken in a 9x13-inch pan. Bake for 30 minutes.

ERMA YODER
Middlefield, OH

ITALIAN CHICKEN

6 boneless chicken breasts
Salt and pepper to taste
6 slices Swiss cheese
1 (10¾ ounce) can of cream of chicken soup
½ cup water
3 tablespoons butter
1 cup bread crumbs (Italian style)

Preheat oven to 375 degrees. Put chicken breasts in 9x13-inch baking pan. Sprinkle with salt and pepper. Top each chicken breast with a slice of cheese. Mix soup and water together and pour over chicken and cheese. Melt butter and mix with bread crumbs. Sprinkle over chicken. Cover and bake for 1½ hours. Uncover for last 20 to 30 minutes.

RACHEL BRICKER
Middlefield, OH

Barbecue Meatballs

3 pounds ground beef
2 cups quick-cooking oats
2 eggs
1 (13 ounce) can evaporated milk
1 cup chopped onion
½ teaspoon garlic powder
2 teaspoons salt
½ teaspoon pepper
2 teaspoons chili pepper

Preheat oven to 350 degrees. Mix all the meat ingredients together and form into balls. Bake in a 9x13-inch baking pan for 30 minutes, uncovered.

Barbeque Sauce:
2 cups ketchup
1 cup brown sugar
1 tablespoon liquid smoke
½ teaspoon garlic powder

Combine all the sauce ingredients and pour over the hot meatballs; cover and bake an additional 30 minutes, or until done.

Mary Alice Yoder
Topeka, IN

Sweet and Sour Spareribs

5 to 6 pounds pork spareribs or pork loin back ribs
½ cup brown sugar
½ cup white sugar
2 tablespoons cornstarch
1 cup ketchup
⅔ cup vinegar
½ cup cold water

Preheat oven to 350 degrees. Place ribs on a rack in a large, shallow roasting pan. Bake ribs uncovered for 1½ hours. Meanwhile, combine the sugars and cornstarch in a medium saucepan. Stir in the ketchup, vinegar, and water. Bring to a boil. Cook and stir until thickened and clear. Remove the ribs and rack from pan and discard fat. Place ribs back in the pan. Pour about 1½ cups of the sauce over the ribs. Bake 30 minutes longer. Cut ribs into serving-size pieces and brush with remaining sauce.

Arlene Wengard
Middlefield, OH

HAYSTACK

½ pound (8 ounces) saltine crackers, crushed
2 cups cooked rice
2 heads lettuce, chopped
2 packages corn chips
6 to 8 tomatoes, chopped
2 cups chopped nuts
1 (6 ounce) can black olives, sliced
3 pounds ground beef, browned
2 eggs, boiled and chopped up
1 (16 ounce) jar Ragu spaghetti sauce or salsa
2 cans cheddar soup
1 (14 ounce) can condensed milk

Put all ingredients into separate containers. Mix soup and milk together in a saucepan and heat. Serve cheese sauce and hamburger warm. Each person will serve up their own plate using items in the order given. Serves 12 to 14 people.

MRS. LEVI SCHWARTZ
Berne, IN

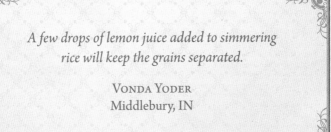

A few drops of lemon juice added to simmering rice will keep the grains separated.

VONDA YODER
Middlebury, IN

POTLUCK POTATOES

2 pounds potatoes (5 medium)
½ cup butter
1 (10¾ ounce) can cream of mushroom soup
1 teaspoon onion salt
¼ teaspoon pepper
1 pint sour cream
2 cups Velveeta processed cheese
1 teaspoon seasoning salt
½ cup butter
2 cups Corn Flakes cereal, crushed
1 teaspoon parsley flakes (optional)
1 teaspoon celery flakes (optional)

Preheat oven to 350 degrees. Slice potatoes and boil in a kettle until almost tender. In another kettle, combine ½ cup butter, soup, onion salt, pepper, sour cream, cheese, and seasoning salt; then heat until cheese is melted. Melt ½ cup butter in a separate saucepan and stir into the crushed corn flakes. Put potatoes in a casserole dish and pour the cheese mixture over them. Cover with the buttered corn flakes. Sprinkle with parsley and celery flakes. Bake for 45 minutes.

ARLENE WENGERD
Middlefield, OH

CHILI PIE CASSEROLE

~~~~~~

3 cups Fritos corn chips, divided
1 large onion, chopped
1 cup shredded cheese, divided
2 cups chili

Preheat oven to 350 degrees. Put 2 cups corn chips in a casserole dish. Put onion and half of cheese over the chips. Pour chili over the cheese. Top with remaining chips and cheese. Bake for 15 to 20 minutes.

SHARON KNEPP
Chouteau, OK

BARBECUE LOADED BAKED POTATO CASSEROLE

2-pound bag Tater Tots
¼ cup margarine or butter
Salt and pepper to taste
1 large onion, chopped
1 (2.5 ounce) package bacon bits, divided
3 cups shredded mozzarella cheese, divided
1 (18 ounce) tub barbecued beef

Preheat oven to 350 degrees. Coat 9x13-inch pan with cooking spray. Put a layer of tots in the bottom. Slice margarine and lay over Tater Tots. Sprinkle with salt and pepper. Spread the onions, half of the bacon bits, and half of cheese on top. Cover with the beef. Heat casserole, covered with foil, for 45 minutes. Remove from oven and add rest of cheese and bacon bits. Heat until cheese is melted. It is good to eat with Ranch dressing.

SHARON KNEPP
Chouteau, OK

Burrito Casserole

2 pounds ground beef, browned
1 (15 ounce) can pork and beans
½ cup brown sugar
1 cup French dressing
1 package taco seasoning
2 (10¾ ounce) cans cream of chicken or mushroom soup
2 cups sour cream
1 package (10 inch) soft tortillas
1 (16 ounce) package shredded cheddar cheese

Preheat oven to 325 degrees. Mix browned beef, beans, sugar, French dressing, and taco seasoning together in a bowl. In a separate bowl, mix soup and sour cream; set aside. Put half of soup mixture on the bottom of 9x13-inch pan. Layer half of tortillas on top of the soup mixture. Put all of hamburger mixture on top of tortillas. Put the rest of tortillas on top. Spread remaining soup mixture over top. Bake for 1 hour. Remove from oven and top with cheddar cheese; return to oven until cheese is melted.

Leona Mullet
Burton, OH

MASHED POTATO CASSEROLE

¾ cup chopped onion
½ cup butter
8 cups cubed ham or any other meat
3 (10¾ ounce) cans cream of mushroom soup
3 cups cubed Velveeta processed cheese
2 tablespoons Worcestershire sauce
¾ teaspoon pepper
6 quarts mashed potatoes (do not add milk or salt)
3 cups sour cream
2 pounds bacon, cut up and fried

Preheat oven to 350 degrees. Sauté onion in butter. Mix onion with ham, soup, cheese, Worcestershire sauce, and pepper together in a bowl. Place in a large roasting pan or casserole dish. In another bowl, mix the potatoes and sour cream; then spread on the meat mixture. Fry cut up bacon and put on top. Bake for 1 hour.

"If I use chicken for this, I like it grilled. Gives it a great taste!"

MARY ROSE YODER
Shipshewana, IN

CHICKEN AND RICE CASSEROLE

1 box Rice-A-Roni long-grain rice
1 small can water chestnuts, chopped
1 small green pepper, chopped
2 cups chopped celery
¼ onion, chopped
1 (10¾ ounce) can cream of chicken soup
1 cup cubed Velveeta processed cheese
1 cup mayonnaise
1 cup chicken broth
2 cups cut up, cooked chicken
2 cups shredded cheese

Preheat oven to 350 degrees. In a large bowl, mix rice, water chestnuts, green pepper, celery, and onion. In a separate bowl, blend soup, cheese, mayonnaise, and broth. Add to rice mixture and fold in chicken. Put into greased 9x13-inch pan. Bake for 30 minutes. Remove from the oven and sprinkle with shredded cheese. Place back in the oven until the cheese is melted.

DORETTA YODER
Topeka, IN

To keep celery crisp, stand it up in a pitcher of cold, salted water and refrigerate.

BARBARA TROYER
Millersburg, OH

CREAMED PEAS

⅛ teaspoon baking soda
⅔ cup water
1 pound frozen peas
1 tablespoon sugar
¾ teaspoon salt

¼ teaspoon black pepper
3 tablespoons butter
¾ cup milk
1½ teaspoon flour

In a saucepan, dissolve baking soda in water and add peas, sugar, salt, and pepper. Bring it to boil; then add butter. Combine milk and flour together in a bowl and stir slowly into the peas. Bring to a boil again and cook over medium heat until thick and bubbly, about 5 minutes.

RACHEL BRICKER
Middlefield, OH

SWEET POTATOES

4 medium size sweet potatoes
⅓ cup flour
4 tablespoons butter
Salt to taste

Preheat oven to 350 degrees. Peel and slice sweet potatoes ½-inch thick. Dip sweet potatoes in flour and then fry in butter (very lightly browned) and salt lightly. To finish cooking, put potatoes on a cookie sheet in the oven uncovered and bake for 15 to 20 minutes or until soft. Serve with extra butter.

RUBY BORNTRAGER
Goshen, IN

SECOND CHRISTMAS

In many Amish communities, December 26th, the day after Christmas, is known as "Second Christmas." While not strictly focused on the religious meaning of the holiday, in many Amish districts it's a day of relaxation and visiting with others. All Amish businesses are closed on that day, and it's a time for families to be with friends and extended family who were not able to be with them on Christmas Day. Sometimes Amish families will hire a driver to take them to another Amish community to visit family or close friends.

Gifts are often exchanged among friends and family members who get together on Second Christmas.

Of course a meal is almost always part of the day, which could be anything from roasted chicken to something simple, like soup and sandwiches. After the meal, everyone gathers around to visit, and various board games are usually played by those who choose to remain in the house. The children will usually go outside for sledding, if there's snow on the ground, or they might play a game of volleyball or baseball if the weather permits.

Second Christmas is basically celebrating Christmas twice, only with a different group of people, and the focus is more on the relaxed, happy occasion.

Old Christmas

Among the Amish, twelve days after Christmas—January 6th—is referred to as "Old Christmas," which for many Amish people, includes morning fasting, followed by dinner at noon. Some Old Order Amish groups put more emphasis on "Old" Christmas than they do on "New" Christmas.

In other Christian traditions, January 6th is called "Epiphany," and it's recognized as the day the three wise men visited Jesus. However, the Amish observe that day because it was the original date of Christmas before the change from the Julian to the Gregorian calendar.

In most Amish communities, Old Christmas is recognized, but as with many other things, this differs in some areas. For those communities that do celebrate Old Christmas, Amish-owned businesses are always closed on January 6th.

Some districts choose to have church on Old Christmas, rather than the Sunday closest to that day. This makes it possible for more visiting ministers to come.

Old Christmas is basically another day available for families and friends to schedule get-togethers, where there will definitely be good food and fellowship.

Regardless of whether an Amish community celebrates Old Christmas or not, they keep their focus on the birth of God's Son and are reminded of Matthew 1:21: *She shall bring forth a son, and thou shalt call his name JESUS: for he shall save his people from their sins.*

> *To every thing there is a season,*
> *and a time to every purpose under the heaven.*
>
> ECCLESIASTES 3:1

Sweets and Desserts

Each day comes bearing its gifts;
all we have to do is untie the ribbons.

Coconut Bon Bons

2 teaspoons coconut flavoring
1 teaspoon vanilla
Pinch of salt
1 (8 ounce) package cream cheese, room temperature
1 pound powdered sugar
10 ounces unsweetened coconut
1 (12 ounce) package chocolate chips, melted for dipping

In a mixing bowl, work coconut flavoring, vanilla, and salt into cream cheese. Mix well. In another bowl, mix powdered sugar and coconut together; then add to cream cheese mixture and stir until well combined. Refrigerate 1 hour or more. Roll into balls and dip into melted chocolate.

MARY MILLER
Shipshewana, IN

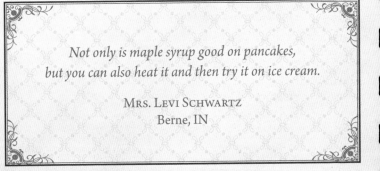

Not only is maple syrup good on pancakes,
but you can also heat it and then try it on ice cream.

MRS. LEVI SCHWARTZ
Berne, IN

FUDGE PUDDLES

½ cup butter
½ cup creamy peanut butter
½ cup sugar
½ cup brown sugar, packed
1 egg
½ teaspoon vanilla
1¼ cup flour
¾ teaspoon baking powder
½ teaspoon salt

Preheat oven to 325 degrees. In a mixing bowl, cream butter, peanut butter, and sugars together. Add egg and vanilla and stir. Then add flour, baking powder, and salt. Mix well. Chill 1 hour. Roll into 48 balls. Place in lightly greased mini muffin tins. Bake for 14 to 16 minutes or until lightly browned. Immediately make a well into the center of each ball by pressing with a melon baller. Cool for 5 minutes. Take out of tins to add filling.

FUDGE FILLING:
1 cup milk chocolate chips
1 cup semi-sweet chocolate chips
1 (14 ounce) can condensed milk
1 teaspoon vanilla

Melt filling ingredients together over low heat, and fill cookie balls.

Optional: Add nuts to filling or use peanut butter cup candies instead of fudge filling.

DORETTA YODER
Topeka, IN

Chocolate Mint Wafers

⅔ cup butter, softened
½ cup sugar
½ cup brown sugar
¼ cup milk
1 egg
2 cups flour
¾ cup baking cocoa
1 teaspoon baking powder
½ teaspoon baking soda
¼ teaspoon salt

Preheat oven to 375 degrees. Cream butter and sugars in a mixing bowl. Add milk and egg; mix well. Combine the flour, cocoa, baking powder, baking soda, and salt and mix well. Gradually add to creamed mixture and mix well. Cover and chill for 2 hours or until firm. Roll chilled dough on a floured surface to ⅛-inch thickness. Cut with 1½-inch round cookie cutter and place 1 inch apart on greased cookie sheet. Bake for 5 to 6 minutes or until edges of cookies are browned. Cool completely.

FILLING:
2¾ cup powdered sugar
¼ teaspoon salt
¼ cup milk
¼ teaspoon peppermint extract
Green food coloring

Mix the filling ingredients together in a bowl and spread on half of the cookies and top with another cookie.

Sadie Bricker
Middlefield, OH

DOUBLE CHOCOLATE TREATS

1 cup butter
1 cup sugar
1 cup brown sugar
2 eggs
½ cup light corn syrup
1 teaspoon vanilla

4 cups flour
½ cup cocoa
2 tablespoons baking soda
1 teaspoon salt
2 cups vanilla chips or Andes mint chips

Preheat oven to 350 degrees. Cream butter and sugars together in mixing bowl. Add eggs, corn syrup, and vanilla and mix well. Add flour, cocoa, baking soda, and salt and stir until combined. Refrigerate for a few hours. Roll into balls and put on a cookie sheet and bake for 10 to 12 minutes or until cracks look dry. Do not over bake or they will be too hard. Melt the vanilla chips or mints and drizzle on the cookies.

LAURA MILLER
Windsor, OH

Chocolate Thumbprints

½ cup butter, softened
⅔ cup sugar
1 egg, separated
2 tablespoons milk
1 teaspoon vanilla

1 cup flour
⅓ cup baking cocoa
¼ teaspoon salt
1 cup finely chopped walnuts

In a mixing bowl, beat butter, sugar, egg yolk, milk, and vanilla until light and fluffy. Combine flour, cocoa, and salt and then gradually add to creamed mixture. Cover and chill for 1 hour or until firm enough to roll into balls.

Preheat oven to 350 degrees. In a smaller bowl, lightly beat the egg white. Roll dough into 1 inch balls; dip in egg white and then roll in nuts. Place 2 inches apart on greased baking sheets. Make an indentation with thumb in center of each cookie. Bake for 10 to 12 minutes or until center is set.

FILLING:

½ cup powdered sugar
1 tablespoon butter, softened
2 teaspoons milk

¼ teaspoon vanilla
24 milk chocolate kisses,
  unwrapped

In a mixing bowl, combine the powdered sugar, butter, milk, and vanilla until smooth. Spoon ¼ teaspoon into each warm cookie and gently press a chocolate kiss in the center. Carefully remove from baking sheet to wire racks to cool completely. Yield: 2 dozen.

SALOMA YODER
Middlefield, OH

GINGER COOKIES

1 cup shortening
½ cup sugar
½ cup molasses
1 egg
1 teaspoon vanilla
2¾ cups flour
¾ teaspoon salt
½ teaspoon baking soda
½ teaspoon baking powder
1 teaspoon ginger
1 teaspoon cinnamon
1 teaspoon cloves

Put shortening and sugar together in a mixing bowl and cream well. Beat in molasses, egg, and vanilla. Sift together dry ingredients and gradually blend into wet mixture. Chill the dough for at least 3 hours.

Preheat oven to 375 degrees. Roll dough out to ⅛- to ¼-inch thickness on a floured surface. Cut cookies with floured cookie cutter. Bake on ungreased cookie sheets for 8 to 10 minutes. Yield: 2 ½ dozen.

ELSIE MAST
Shiloh, OH

BUTTER CUT-OUT COOKIES

1 cup butter, softened
2 cups white sugar
2 eggs
1 cup sour cream
2 teaspoons vanilla
2 teaspoons baking soda
1 teaspoon salt
7 cups flour

Preheat oven to 375 degrees. In a mixing bowl, cream butter and sugar together. Add eggs, sour cream, and vanilla and mix well. In a separate bowl, combine baking soda, salt, and flour, and mix into wet mixture. Roll dough out on flat, floured surface and cut out cookies or press teaspoons of dough flat on cookie sheet. Bake for 8 to 10 minutes. Don't bake until brown. They should still be white. Frost cookies when cool.

FROSTING:
½ cup milk
1 (3 ounce) box instant vanilla pudding
½ cup butter, softened (no substitute)
5 cups powdered sugar
2 teaspoons vanilla
Food coloring (optional)

In a bowl, combine milk and pudding mix and beat until smooth. Cream butter in another bowl, and gradually add pudding mixture. Then add powdered sugar, vanilla, and food coloring if desired. Beat until light and fluffy.

DIANNA YODER
Goshen, IN

PUMPKIN WHOOPIE PIES

2 cups brown sugar
1 cup vegetable oil
1½ cup pumpkin (cooked or canned)
2 eggs
1 teaspoon vanilla
3 cups flour
1 teaspoon salt
1 teaspoon baking powder
1 teaspoon baking soda
1½ tablespoon cinnamon
½ tablespoon cloves
½ tablespoon ginger

Preheat oven to 350 degrees. Cream sugar and oil together in mixing bowl. Add pumpkin, eggs, and vanilla and mix well. Add rest of dry ingredients and stir until combined. Drop by a heaping teaspoon onto greased cookie sheet. Bake for 10 to 12 minutes.

FILLING:
2 egg whites
1½ cup shortening
1 teaspoon vanilla
¼ teaspoon salt
4½ cups powdered sugar

In a bowl, beat egg whites and add shortening, vanilla, and salt until combined. Stir in the powdered sugar and mix until creamy. Put this filling on a cookie and then put another cookie on top. Wrap them each in Saran Wrap.

IRENE MILLER
Shipshewana, IN

SPECIAL K CHEWIES

◇◇

½ cup light corn syrup
½ cup sugar
2 cups Special K or corn flakes cereal
⅔ cup peanut butter
1 teaspoon vanilla

In a saucepan, boil syrup and sugar together just long enough to dissolve the sugar. Remove from heat and add Special K, peanut butter, and vanilla. Drop by a teaspoon on waxed paper.

MARY AND KATIE YODER
Goshen, IN

PEANUT BLOSSOMS

½ cup shortening
½ cup peanut butter
1 egg
2 tablespoons milk
1 teaspoon vanilla
1¾ cup flour
½ cup white sugar
½ cup brown sugar
1 teaspoon soda
½ teaspoon salt
24 to 30 milk chocolate kisses

Preheat oven to 375 degrees. Cream shortening, peanut butter, egg, milk, and vanilla together in a bowl. Add flour, sugars, soda, and salt and mix well. Shape into walnut-size balls and place on ungreased cookie sheet. Bake for 10 to 12 minutes. Remove from oven and top each cookie immediately with a candy kiss, pressing down firmly so cookie cracks around the edge.

IDA TROYER
Burton, OH

No Bake Chocolate Cookies

2 cups sugar
½ cup milk
¼ teaspoon salt
4 teaspoons cocoa
½ cup margarine
½ cup crunchy peanut butter
1 teaspoon vanilla
3 cups oats

In a medium saucepan, mix sugar, milk, salt, cocoa, and margarine,
and cook for 1½ minutes after it starts to boil. Remove from
heat and add peanut butter and vanilla. Then stir in oats. Drop by
spoonful onto pan lined with wax paper or press onto cookie sheet.
Yield: 2 dozen.

VONDA YODER
Middlebury, IN

HOLIDAY SPRITZ

1 cup butter, softened
1 cup powdered sugar
1 egg
1½ teaspoon vanilla
2½ cups flour
¼ teaspoon salt
Colored sugar sprinkles

Preheat oven to 375 degrees. In a mixing bowl, cream butter and powdered sugar until light and fluffy. Beat in egg and vanilla. In a separate bowl, combine flour and salt; gradually add to creamed mixture and mix well. Using a cookie press, press cookies 1 inch apart on ungreased baking sheets. Sprinkle with colored sugar sprinkles. Bake for 6 to 9 minutes. Cool for 2 minutes before removing to wire racks.

SADIE BRICKER
Middlefield, OH

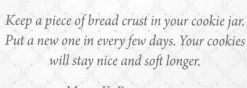

Keep a piece of bread crust in your cookie jar.
Put a new one in every few days. Your cookies
will stay nice and soft longer.

MARY K. BONTRAGER
Middlebury, IN

CHOCOLATE TRUFFLE COOKIES

1¼ cup butter, softened
⅓ cup cocoa
2¼ cups powdered sugar
⅓ cup heavy cream
2¼ cups flour
2 cups semi-sweet chocolate chips

Cream butter, cocoa, and powdered sugar in a mixing bowl until fluffy. Beat in cream. Add flour and mix well. Stir in chocolate chips. Refrigerate for 1 hour. Preheat oven to 325 degrees. Form 1-inch balls and put on ungreased cookie sheet. Bake for 10 minutes, until just set. Do not over bake! Cool 5 minutes before removing from baking sheet.

SHARON KNEPP
Chouteau, OK

Peanut Butter Fingers

1 cup white sugar
1 cup brown sugar
1 cup shortening
¾ cup peanut butter
2 eggs
2 teaspoons vanilla
1 teaspoon salt
1 teaspoon soda
2 cups flour
2 cups oats
1 cup chocolate chips

Preheat oven to 350 degrees. Cream sugars, shortening, and peanut butter together in a mixing bowl. Add eggs and vanilla and stir well. Stir in salt, soda, flour, and oats and then mix well. Press onto greased cookie sheet and bake for 30 to 35 minutes. When baked, sprinkle chocolate chips over the top and let set for 5 minutes. With a knife, spread the soft chocolate chips over the bars. Let cool and then frost.

Frosting:
2 cups powdered sugar
½ cup peanut butter
4 tablespoons milk

In a bowl, mix ingredients together until creamy and spread over top of the bars. When frosting is set, cut into bars.

Irene Miller
Shipshewana, IN

ITALIAN SPRINKLE COOKIES

6 eggs
5 cups flour
2 cups powdered sugar
2 tablespoons plus 1½ teaspoon baking powder
1 cup vegetable oil
1 tablespoon almond extract
1½ teaspoon lemon extract

Preheat oven to 350 degrees. In a mixing bowl, beat eggs until light and foamy, about 5 minutes. Set aside. In another mixing bowl, combine flour, sugar, and baking powder. Stir in oil and extracts. Gradually add eggs. Roll dough into 1-inch balls. Place them on ungreased baking sheets. Bake for 12 minutes. As soon as cookies are removed from oven, quickly immerse two at a time into glaze. Remove with slotted spoon. Place cookies on wire racks to drain. Quickly top with sprinkles. Let dry 24 hours before storing in airtight containers.

GLAZE:
½ cup warm milk
1 teaspoon almond extract
1 teaspoon vanilla extract
3¾ cup powdered sugar
Colored sprinkles

Combine milk and extracts in a large bowl. Add powdered sugar and whisk until glaze is smooth. Proceed as noted above.

ERMA YODER
Middlefield, OH

Peanut Butter Sandwich Cookies

1 cup margarine
1 cup peanut butter
1 cup white sugar
1 cup brown sugar
3 eggs, beaten
1 teaspoon vanilla
3 cups flour
½ teaspoon salt
2 teaspoons baking soda

Preheat oven to 375 degrees. Cream margarine, peanut butter, and sugars together in a mixing bowl. Add eggs and vanilla. Combine flour, salt, and soda, and add to the cream mixture. Mix well. Roll into balls, place on ungreased cookie sheet, and flatten with a fork. Bake for 8 to 10 minutes. Cool and put frosting in between 2 cookies.

FROSTING:
½ cup peanut butter
6 tablespoons milk
1 teaspoon vanilla
3 cups powdered sugar

Combine all ingredients together and mix until creamy.

MARY BONTRAGER
Middlebury, IN

EASY TIME HOLIDAY SQUARES

1 cup butter, softened
1½ cup white sugar
4 eggs
1 tablespoon lemon juice
2 cups flour
1 (21 ounce) can pie filling
Powdered sugar

Preheat oven to 350 degrees. Cream butter and sugar in a mixing bowl. Add eggs, one at a time. Add lemon juice and flour. Mix well. Spread batter in greased jelly roll pan. With toothpick, mark off 20 squares. Add tablespoon of pie filling into each square. Bake for 45 to 50 minutes. When done, sift powdered sugar over squares.

LAURA MILLER
Windsor, OH

Fudgy Chocolate Cookie Bars

1¾ cup flour
¾ cup powdered sugar
¼ cup baking cocoa
1 cup margarine
1 (12 ounce) package chocolate chips, divided
1 (14 ounce) can condensed milk
1 teaspoon vanilla
1 cup chopped nuts

Preheat oven to 350 degrees. In a bowl, mix together flour, sugar, and cocoa. Cut in margarine until crumbly. Press into bottom of 9x13-inch pan. Bake for 15 minutes. In a saucepan, melt 1 cup chocolate chips with milk and vanilla. Pour over crust. Top with nuts and remaining chocolate chips. Bake for 20 minutes more. Cool. Cut into squares.

Leona Mullet
Burton, OH

PINEAPPLE OATMEAL COOKIE BARS

¼ cup white sugar
1 tablespoon corn starch
1 cup crushed pineapple
1 teaspoon lemon juice
1 cup flour
1 teaspoon salt
1 cup brown sugar
2½ cups oats
1 cup shortening

Preheat oven to 350 degrees. In a saucepan, combine white sugar and cornstarch. Add pineapple (do not drain) and cook slowly until thick and clear. Add lemon juice and cool. In a bowl, sift flour and salt; then add the brown sugar and oats and stir. Add shortening and cut in until crumbly. Press ½ of mixture in greased 7x11-inch baking pan. Spread with pineapple mixture. Sprinkle with remaining crumbs over the top, patting smooth. Bake for 45 minutes.

BARBARA TROYER
Millersburg, OH

KRISPIE CARAMEL BARS

¼ cup butter
4 cups marshmallows
4 cups Rice Krispies cereal
14 ounces caramels
1 stick butter
1 (14 ounce) can condensed milk

Melt butter and marshmallows together in a saucepan. Add Rice
Krispies and press half of mixture in greased 9x13-inch pan. In a
saucepan, melt caramels, butter, and milk together till smooth and
pour over the first layer. Repeat with the other half of the first layer.
Refrigerate.

IDA TROYER
Burton, OH

CRACKED ICE PUDDING

1 small box lime gelatin
1 small box lemon gelatin
1 small box grape gelatin
2 small boxes orange gelatin
6 cups boiling water, divided
2 cups heavy whipping cream

In separate mixing bowls, prepare lime, lemon, and grape gelatins individually with 1 cup of boiling water each. Pour each into separate pans and refrigerate until set. Mix orange gelatin with 3 cups boiling water and chill until it starts to set. Whip cream till it stands in peaks. Add the whipped cream to the orange gelatin. Cut other gelatins in squares and add to whipped mixture. Chill and serve.

WILMA HASTON
Greenwich, OH

DATE PUDDING

1 cup dates, chopped
1 teaspoon soda
1 tablespoon butter
1 cup boiling water
1 cup sugar
1 egg
1¼ cup flour
½ cup nuts
1 (8 ounce) tub whipped topping

Preheat oven to 350 degrees. Put dates, soda, and butter in a bowl and pour hot water over all. Cool. Add sugar, egg, flour, and nuts and mix well. Put into greased 8x8-inch baking pan and bake for 30 minutes or until done. Cool. Cut in squares and put in a bowl; pour sauce over it and top with whipped topping.

SAUCE:
½ cup butter
1 cup brown sugar
2 cups water
¼ cup ClearJel (or 3 tablespoons cornstarch)
⅛ teaspoon salt
1 teaspoon vanilla

Brown butter in a saucepan; then add brown sugar and stir until bubbly. Add water, bring to a boil, and thicken with ClearJel or cornstarch. Add salt and vanilla. Cool.

RACHEL YODER
Burton, OH

BUTTERSCOTCH TAPIOCA

6 cups water
1 teaspoon salt
1½ cup tapioca
2 cups brown sugar
2 eggs, beaten
1 cup milk
½ cup white sugar
1 stick butter
1 teaspoon vanilla
1 (8 ounce) whipped topping
Candy bars of your choice (optional)
Bananas (optional)

In a large pot, bring water and salt to a boil; add tapioca and cook for 15 minutes. Add brown sugar and cook until tapioca is done. Stir often. Mix eggs, milk, and white sugar together and add to tapioca and cook until bubbles form. In a saucepan, brown butter and add to tapioca along with vanilla. Cool completely before adding whipped topping. Optional: Diced candy bars of your choice and/or sliced bananas can be added.

IRENE MILLER
Shipshewana, IN

CRACKER PUDDING

2 cups milk
¾ cup sugar
¼ cup cornstarch
⅛ teaspoon salt
2 egg yolks, beaten
2 tablespoons butter
1 teaspoon vanilla
1 (8 ounce) tub whipped topping
1 package graham crackers, crushed
¼ cup sugar
¼ cup butter

In a saucepan, bring milk to a boil. Combine ¾ cup sugar, cornstarch, salt, egg yolks, and enough hot milk to blend ingredients together. Stir mixture into the milk pan and stir over heat until thickened. Remove from heat and add 2 tablespoons butter and vanilla. Cool completely. Stir in half of whipped topping. Crush graham crackers and add ¼ cup sugar. Melt ¼ cup butter and mix into the cracker crumbs. Layer pudding and cracker mixture into a bowl and top with rest of whipped topping. Optional: Crushed cinnamon graham crackers, Corn Chex cereal, or Oreo cookies can be used instead of regular graham cracker crumbs.

LEONA MULLET
Burton, OH

PECAN PUMPKIN DESSERT

2 (15 ounce) cans pumpkin
1 (12 ounce) can evaporated milk
1 cup sugar
3 eggs, beaten
1 teaspoon vanilla
1 (18¼ ounce) package yellow or butter pecan cake mix
1 cup butter, melted
1½ cup chopped pecans

Preheat oven to 350 degrees. Line 9x13-inch baking pan with waxed paper. Coat pan with non-stick cooking spray. Set aside. In a mixing bowl, combine pumpkin, milk, sugar, eggs, and vanilla and mix well. Pour into prepared pan. Sprinkle pumpkin mixture with dry cake mix and drizzle with melted butter. Sprinkle pecans over the top. Bake for 1 hour and cool completely in the pan. Invert onto large serving platter and remove wax paper. Cover with frosting.

FROSTING:
1 (8 ounce) package cream cheese, softened
1½ cup powdered sugar
1 teaspoon vanilla
1 (8 ounce) tub whipped topping

In a mixing bowl, beat cream cheese, sugar, and vanilla until smooth. Fold in whipped topping and frost dessert. Store dessert in the refrigerator.

MARY ROSE YODER
Shipshewana, IN

CHOCOLATE AND FRUIT TRUFFLE

1 package chocolate cake mix
1 (14 ounce) can sweetened condensed milk
1 cup cold water
2 tablespoons lemon juice
1 small (3.4 oz) package instant vanilla pudding
2 cups whipped topping
2 cups fresh strawberries, chopped or sliced
2 cups kiwifruit, peeled and chopped
2 cups raspberries

Preheat oven to 350 degrees. Prepare cake according to directions and bake. When cool, crumble cake. In a separate mixing bowl, combine milk, water, and lemon juice and add pudding mix. Beat until slightly thickened. Fold in whipped topping. Put pudding, crumbled cake, and fruit in layers in a glass bowl.

ARLENE WENGERD
Middlefield, OH

White Cloud Dessert

8 egg whites
1 teaspoon cream of tarter
1¼ cup sugar
1 (8 ounce) package cream cheese
1 cup powdered sugar
1 teaspoon vanilla
1 (8 ounce) tub whipped topping
1 (21 ounce) can fruit pie filling (of your choice)

Preheat oven to 200 degrees. In a bowl, beat egg whites till foamy; then add the cream of tartar. Beat again till soft peaks form. Then add 1 tablespoon sugar at a time and beat until hard peaks form. Spread on ungreased oven-safe serving platter. Bake for 1½ hours. Let cool in oven till completely cooled (about 2 hours). In a mixing bowl, combine cream cheese, sugar, and vanilla together. Then add the whipped topping. Spread the filling over the middle of the baked egg whites and then spread the fruit pie topping over that.

ANNA RUTH ESCH
Lykens, PA

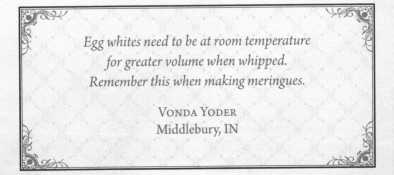

Egg whites need to be at room temperature
for greater volume when whipped.
Remember this when making meringues.

VONDA YODER
Middlebury, IN

EASY BLUEBERRY DESSERT

1 (8 ounce) package cream cheese
1 (12 ounce) tub whipped topping
1 (14 ounce) can sweetened condensed milk
1 quart (4 cups) blueberry pie filling
1 (20 ounce) can pineapple chunks, drained

Mix cream cheese, whipped topping, and milk together in a bowl. Add pie filling and pineapple. Mix all together and put in a bowl. Let set up in refrigerator 3 to 4 hours before serving.

MARY BONTRAGER
Middlebury, IN

FROZEN STRAWBERRY DESSERT

1 (8 ounce) package cream cheese
⅔ cup white sugar
1 (8 ounce) tub whipped topping
2 cups cut or chopped strawberries
2 cups small marshmallows

Combine all ingredients together in mixing bowl. Put into container to freeze. When ready to use, take out of freezer 10 minutes before serving.

MARY BONTRAGER
Middlebury, IN

Orange Pineapple Ice Cream

2 small boxes vanilla instant pudding
4 eggs, well beaten
3 cups sugar
1 large box orange gelatin, dissolved in 1 cup boiling water
2 cups heavy whipping cream
½ cup pineapple juice
Milk, enough to fill a 1½ gallon ice cream freezer

In a mixing bowl, combine pudding, eggs, sugar, dissolved and cooled gelatin, whipping cream, and pineapple juice together and put in 1½ gallon freezer. Add enough milk to fill freezer, and then freeze according to freezer directions, using ice and rock salt.

Lovina Miller
Shipshewana, IN

CRANBERRY DESSERT

3 (3 ounce) boxes of gelatin (one each of cherry, orange, and
   raspberry)
¾ cup sugar
3 cups boiling water
1½ cups cold water
2 oranges, chunked
2 apples, chopped
1 small can crushed pineapple
1 (12 ounce) bag cranberries, finely chopped
1½ cup seedless grapes, cut in half
2 stalks celery, cut fine

Mix all gelatins and sugar together in a bowl. Add boiling water and
dissolve. Add cold water and refrigerate until it is soft set. Add all
fruits and celery; mix and let set.

RACHEL YODER
Burton, OH

CRANBERRY DELIGHT

1 (12 ounce) package cranberries
½ cup sugar
1 (20 ounce) can crushed pineapple, drained
1½ (10.5 ounce) packages mini marshmallows, divided
4 ounces cream cheese, softened
1 pint heavy whipping cream, whipped until it forms peaks

Grind up cranberries, add sugar, and set aside. Combine drained pineapple and 1 full package of marshmallows and set aside. In a mixing bowl, combine softened cream cheese with whipped cream; add ½ package marshmallows and then cranberries and pineapple/marshmallows mixture. Put in 9x13-inch pan. Refrigerate.

KATHRYN YODER
Burton, OH

PECAN PIE COBBLER

2 (9 inch) pie crusts, unbaked
2½ cups light corn syrup
2½ cups brown sugar, packed
½ cup butter, melted
4½ teaspoons vanilla
6 eggs, slightly beaten
2 cups coarsely chopped pecans
2 cups pecan halves
Vanilla ice cream, if desired

Preheat oven to 425 degrees. Grease glass 9x13-inch pan with shortening or cooking spray. Roll 1 pie crust into 9x13-inch rectangle; trim sides to fit bottom of baking dish. Place crust in prepared pan. In a mixing bowl, whisk together corn syrup, brown sugar, butter, vanilla, and eggs. Stir in chopped pecans. Spoon half of filling into pie crust. Roll second pie crust into 9x13-inch rectangle; trim sides to fit into baking dish. Place crust over filling. Spray crust with butter-flavor cooking spray. Bake for 14 to 16 minutes or until browned. Reduce oven temperature to 350 degrees. Carefully spoon remaining filling over baked pastry; arrange pecan halves on top. Bake 30 minutes longer or until set. Cool for 20 minutes on cooling rack. Serve warm with ice cream if desired.

SALOMA YODER
Middlefield, OH

MINT BROWNIE PIE

BROWNIE LAYER:

6 tablespoons butter
2 (1 ounce) squares chocolate, unsweetened
1 cup sugar

2 eggs, beaten
½ teaspoon vanilla
½ cup flour

Preheat oven to 350 degrees. In a saucepan, melt butter and chocolate. Stir in sugar until well blended. Add eggs and vanilla. Mix well. Stir in flour until well blended. Pour into greased 9-inch springform pan. Bake for 18 to 20 minutes or until toothpick inserted in the middle comes out clean. Cool.

FILLING:

1 (8 ounce) package cream cheese
¾ cup sugar
½ teaspoon peppermint extract

A few drops green food coloring (optional)
1 (8 ounce) tub whipped topping

In a mixing bowl, beat cream cheese and sugar until smooth. Add extract and food coloring. Mix well. Fold in whipped topping. Spread evenly over cooled brownie layer. Cover and refrigerate at least 1 hour. Remove sides of pan just before serving along with topping.

TOPPING:

1 (8 ounce) tub whipped topping (optional)
¼ cup semi-sweet chocolate chips

Garnish with whipped topping, if desired. Melt chocolate chips and drizzle over top.

ARLENE WENGERD
Middlefield, OH

SOUR CREAM LEMON PIE

1 cup sugar
3½ tablespoons cornstarch
½ cup fresh lemon juice
3 egg yolks
1 cup milk
¼ cup butter
1 cup sour cream
1 baked pie crust
2 cups whipped topping

Combine sugar, cornstarch, lemon juice, egg yolks, and milk in heavy saucepan. Cook over medium heat until thick. Stir in butter until melted. Cool to room temperature. Stir in sour cream. Pour filling into pie shell and cover with whipped topping.

MELVIN AND LEANNA YODER
Shipshewana, IN

FROZEN PEANUT BUTTER PIE

1 (8 ounce) package cream cheese
1 cup peanut butter
1 cup powdered sugar
½ cup milk
1 (8 ounce) tub whipped topping
1 graham cracker pie crust

In a mixing bowl, beat cream cheese till fluffy. Add peanut butter and sugar; then slowly add milk. Fold in whipped topping and pour into pie crust. Cover and freeze several hours. Remove from freezer 10 minutes before serving.

WILMA HASTON
Greenwich, OH

CHOCOLATE TURTLE PIE

2 cups chocolate sandwich cookie crumbs
¼ cup butter
1 cup caramel candies (about 20)
¼ cup whipped topping
½ pound (2 cups) pecan pieces
¾ cup chocolate chips
¼ cup whipped topping

Preheat oven to 375 degrees. Combine cookie crumbs and butter in mixing bowl. Press evenly in bottom and up sides of 9-inch pie plate. Bake 10 minutes. Cool. Melt caramels in heavy saucepan over low heat, stirring often. Stir in ¼ cup whipped topping and nuts. Spread over cookie crumb crust. Refrigerate 15 minutes. Melt chocolate chips and add ¼ cup whipped topping. Drizzle over caramel mixture. Refrigerate for 1 hour.

BETTY BRICKER
Middlefield, OH

PEANUT BUTTER CUP PIE

1 ½ cup white sugar
3 tablespoons flour
3 tablespoons cocoa
¾ cup milk
3 eggs, beaten
1½ teaspoon vanilla
2 (9 inch) unbaked pie shells

Preheat oven to 350 degrees. Mix sugar, flour, cocoa, milk, eggs, and vanilla together in a bowl, and pour into 2 unbaked pie shells. Bake for 30 minutes or until set. Cool.

TOPPING:
1 (8 ounce) package cream cheese, softened
1 cup powdered sugar
½ cup peanut butter
2 (8 ounce) tubs of whipped topping
1 teaspoon vanilla
Grated chocolate
Peanut butter cup candy, cut in pieces

In a bowl, combine cream cheese and powdered sugar well; then add peanut butter, vanilla, and first tub of whipped topping. Put on top of chilled chocolate-filled pies. Cover pies using second tub of whipped topping. Grated chocolate or pieces of peanut butter cup candy may be sprinkled over top.

MARY ROSE YODER
Shipshewana, IN

Fluffy Yogurt Pie

1 (8 ounce) package cream cheese
1 (14 ounce) can condensed milk
1 (8 ounce) strawberry yogurt
2 teaspoons lemon juice
2 teaspoons red food coloring (optional)
1 (8 ounce) tub whipped topping
1 (9 inch) baked pie crust

In a large bowl, beat cream cheese until fluffy. Gradually add milk until smooth. Stir in yogurt, lemon juice, and food coloring. Fold in whipped topping and pour into prepared crust. Chill for 4 hours.

Rachel Yoder
Burton, OH

When making cream pies, sprinkle the crusts with powdered sugar in order to prevent them from becoming soggy.

Barbara Troyer
Millersburg, OH

Oatmeal Pecan Pie

<><><><><><><><><><><><><><><><><><><><><><><><><><><><><><><><><><><><><><><><>

3 cups brown sugar
3 cups oats
3 cups corn syrup
1 pound (2 cups) butter, melted
8 eggs, beaten
2 cups chopped pecans
4 (9 inch) unbaked pie crusts

Preheat oven to 325 degrees. Mix brown sugar, oats, syrup, butter, eggs, and pecans together in a bowl. Pour into 4 unbaked 9-inch pie crusts. Bake for 30 minutes on top shelf and 30 minutes on the bottom shelf.

Linda Miller
Humboldt, IL

MILLIONAIRE PIE

2 cups powdered sugar, not sifted
1 stick butter, softened
1 egg
¼ teaspoon salt
¼ teaspoon vanilla
2 (9 inch) baked pie shells
1 cup heavy whipping cream
1 cup well-drained crushed pineapple
½ cup pecans

Cream powdered sugar and butter in mixing bowl. Add egg, salt, and vanilla; mix well until fluffy. Spread mixture in 2 baked pie shells. In another bowl, whip cream until stiff. Blend in well-drained pineapple and nuts. Spoon this on top of sugar and butter mixture and chill.

MRS. LEVI SCHWARTZ
Berne, IN

VANILLA TART PIE

1 cup dark corn syrup
1 egg
1 cup sugar
2 tablespoons flour
2 cups cold water
4 (9 inch) unbaked pie crusts

Preheat oven to 400 degrees. In a saucepan, combine syrup, egg, sugar, flour, and water. Cook until thickened (about 8 to 10 minutes). Pour into 4 unbaked pie crusts.

TOPPING:
2 cups sugar
2 eggs
1 cup sour milk
½ cup butter
1 tablespoon soda
2½ cups flour

Mix sugar, eggs, sour milk, butter, soda, and flour together in a bowl, then put on top by spoonfuls. Bake at 400 degrees for 5 minutes then at 375 degrees for 8 to 10 minutes, or until done.

IVA YODER
Goshen, IN

GRANDMA'S CHRISTMAS CAKE

½ cup milk
1 teaspoon salt
1 tablespoon sugar
1 package yeast
1 egg
1 tablespoon shortening, soft
2 to 2¼ cups flour, sifted
1 cup mixed dried fruit

Preheat oven to 350 degrees. Grease 2 loaf pans and set aside. Heat milk to lukewarm in medium-sized saucepan. Remove from heat and stir in salt and sugar. Crumble yeast into mixture; stir until dissolved. Stir in egg and shortening. Mix in just enough flour to handle easily. Stir in dried fruit, shape into loaves, and let rise. Bake for 45 minutes.

GLAZE:
2 cups powdered sugar
1 teaspoon vanilla
Water, enough to make frosting drizzle

Combine ingredients and drizzle over loaves when cool.

SADIE BRICKER
Middlefield, OH

WHITE FRUIT CAKE

½ pound (1 cup) butter
1 cup sugar
5 eggs, beaten
1 pound candied cherries
1 pound candied pineapple
4 cups coarsely chopped pecans
2 cups flour, sifted and divided
2 tablespoons vanilla extract
2 tablespoons lemon extract

Prepare 2 tube pans with greased waxed paper or just grease pans well. In a mixing bowl, cream butter well; add sugar and cream until fluffy. Beat eggs well and blend with creamed mixture. Chop cherries, pineapple, and pecans and mix well with small amount of flour and set aside. Sift remaining flour and fold into creamed mixture. Add extracts and fold in fruits and nuts. Pour batter into pans and put into cold oven; then set to 300 degrees. Bake for 1½ hours or until done. Cake can be frozen.

RACHEL YODER
Burton, OH

CHRISTMAS CAKE

1 box white cake mix
1 small package each of red and green gelatin
2 cups boiling water

Preheat oven to 300 degrees. Mix cake mix as directed on box. Cut wax paper to fit bottom of 2 8-inch round pans, and grease paper and pans well. Fill pans with batter. Bake for 40 minutes or until done. Cool. Prick cakes with fork and leave in pans. Mix red gelatin with 1 cup boiling water. Carefully pour dissolved red gelatin over one of the cakes. In another bowl, mix green gelatin with 1 cup boiling water and pour dissolved green gelatin over the other cake. Refrigerate overnight or for a few hours. Take cakes out of pans using spatula and put on plate one at a time, putting frosting between layers.

FROSTING:
1 (8 ounce) package cream cheese, softened
2 (8 ounce) tubs whipped topping

In a bowl, combine cream cheese and one tub whipped topping together. Put between layers of cake. Frost the cake with whipped topping. Decorate, if you wish.

KATHRYN YODER
Burton, OH

Angel Food Cake

2¼ cups egg whites, room temperature
¼ teaspoon salt
1½ teaspoon cream of tartar
1⅓ cups sugar
½ teaspoon almond flavoring or any flavoring
1½ cups cake flour
½ cup sugar
1 small package gelatin, any flavor (optional)

Preheat oven to 375 degrees. In a mixing bowl, beat egg whites until stiff with salt and cream of tartar. Then beat in 1⅓ cup sugar until it holds soft peaks. Fold in flavoring. Sift 1½ cups cake flour and ½ cup sugar together and fold into egg whites with a spoon. Optional: Add dry gelatin and fold in for nice color and different flavor. Bake in ungreased tube pan for 35 minutes. Cool completely before removing.

FROSTING:
1 (8 ounce) package cream cheese
2 cups powdered sugar
1 cup heavy whipping cream

In a bowl, combine cream cheese and powdered sugar and mix well. In a separate bowl, whip cream until stiff and fold into cream cheese mixture. Spread on cake.

SAUCE:
1 tablespoon instant ClearJel (can be found in bulk stores)
2 tablespoons sugar
1 pint strawberries, chopped

Mix ClearJel and sugar together and slowly add strawberries, stirring constantly. (This is not to be heated.) When thickened, put on top of frosted cake and let drip down the sides. (You can use any thickened fruit on top of cake.)

LYDIA MILLER
Goshen, IN

Peppermint Cheesecake

15 to 20 Oreo cookies, crushed
¼ cup butter, melted
1 (14 ounce) can sweetened condensed milk
1 (8 ounce) package cream cheese, softened
1 cup sour cream
1 (12 ounce) tub whipped topping
2 to 3 drops peppermint flavoring
3 large candy canes, crushed (save some for garnish)

In a bowl, mix Oreo cookies and butter together and press in 13x9-inch pan. In another bowl, mix milk and cream cheese together and add sour cream, whipped topping, flavoring, and crushed candy canes. Pour over crust and garnish with remaining candy cane crumbs. Freeze. Thaw 15 minutes before serving.

Sharon Knepp
Chouteau, OK

ENTERTAINMENT AND GAMES

During the holiday season, some Amish women gather to make cookies and spend time visiting with one another. Many children enjoy wrapping gifts together and making Christmas cards, while their mother and older siblings bake several kinds of pies, sweet rolls, and cookies to share with their friends and neighbors.

Amish children and young people enjoy the time they spend together when they go Christmas caroling. It's fun to sing to their neighbors and friends, and it makes for a nice outing as they share the Good News.

In areas where it snows around Christmastime, the children will often go sledding or ice skating with their friends. Throwing snowballs or making snowmen are also fun pastimes during the cold, holiday weather. Some Amish who own sleighs may take their family for a sleigh ride during snowy weather.

Indoor table games such as Rook, Settlers of Catan, Dutch Blitz, Monopoly, and Apples to Apples are also enjoyed by young and old alike. Some sort of snack, like a bowl of popcorn, pretzels, or potato chips, usually accompanies the games, along with a cold or hot beverage. Some Amish families enjoy reading or putting puzzles together on a cold wintry day.

Regardless of the activities the adults and children take part in, all Amish parents want their family to focus on the religious significance of Christmas.

INDEX

SNACKS AND BITES

BREADS AND ROLLS

Gifts from the Kitchen

Salads, Main Dishes, and Sides

Sweets and Desserts

A *New York Times* bestselling author, WANDA E. BRUNSTETTER became fascinated with the Amish way of life when she first visited her husband's Mennonite relatives living in Pennsylvania. Wanda and her husband, Richard, live in Washington State but take every opportunity to visit Amish settlements throughout the States, where they have many Amish friends.

Let's Keep in Touch!

Want to know what Wanda's up to and be the first to hear about new releases, specials, the latest news, and more? Like Wanda on Facebook!

 Visit facebook.com/WandaBrunstetterFans